Mastering IBM i Security
A Modern Step-by-Step Guide

Carol Woodbury

MC Press Online, LLC
Boise, ID 83703 USA

Mastering IBM i Security: A Modern Step-by-Step Guide

Carol Woodbury

First Printing—July 2022

© Copyright 2022 Carol Woodbury. All rights reserved.

MC Press offers excellent discounts on this book when ordered in quantity for bulk purchases or special sales, which may include custom covers and content particular to your business, training goals, marketing focus, and branding interest.

MC Press Online, LLC
Corporate Offices: 3695 W. Quail Heights Court, Boise, ID 83703-3861 USA
Sales and Customer Service: (208) 629-7275 ext. 500; service@mcpressonline.com
Permissions and Bulk/Special Orders: operations@mcpressonline.com
www.mcpressonline.com • www.mc-store.com

ISBN: 978-1-58347-900-1

To my great-nieces Aliyah, Blake, and Callen

You literally got me through the pandemic.
Without your sweet smiles, hugs, and laughter,
I'm not sure what I would have done.
Each of you is beautiful through and through.
My prayer for you is that you will know Jesus.
And that you will find comfort in His love
when the world is crazy or unfair.
I love you more than you can imagine
and am so thankful to be a part of your lives.

Acknowledgements

First, I could not have written this book without inspiration from Scott Forstie, DB2 for i Business Architect at IBM Rochester. He inspired me to start looking at the IBM i Services for managing security. Using the examples he presented and wrote about, I started to use SQL with my clients, and I haven't looked back. He's generous with sharing his technical expertise and has provided some of the SQL examples in this book. He has a gracious spirit and a tremendous sense of humor. Thank you, Scott, for making this a better book!

My sincere thanks go out to:
The DB2 for i team for all of the SQL enhancements and services you send out with each IBM i operating system release and Technology Refresh. Your work is the basis for this book.

The IBM i Security Team for continuing to provide new features and maintaining a sound basis for securing the system. Special shout-out to Carol Budnik and Barb Smith. You rock!

Tim Rowe and his team for undertaking the huge task of developing New Nav to get us off of Old Nav (sorry, the correct term is "Heritage Nav," but let's face it, Old Nav was OLD!). They've delivered a new and significantly improved user experience with New Nav.

Margaret Fenlon for providing me with information regarding the IBM i 7.5 changes in the IFS and NetServer and for delivering these fantastic enhancements!

Larry Bolhuis, Frankeni Technology Consulting, for access to an IBM i 7.5 partition.

Alison Butterill, Worldwide Program Director, Product Management, IBM i, for enabling early access and for being a great friend for so many years!

Victoria Mack, my longtime editor, for making sense out of my writing and making it readable! If you can understand the concepts I'm trying to convey with my writing, it's because of her. She's taught me so much about writing over the years.

David Uptmor, my longtime publisher, for believing in the concept of this book.

Kara Keating-Stuart for the beautiful cover and artwork.

Finally, I'd be remiss if I didn't thank John Vanderwall, my business partner of 20+ years, for his support. Not only does he know how to start and run a business but he's a great listener and friend. Thanks, pardner.

Introduction

Welcome to my world! I've written this book to provide you with knowledge and insight that I've gained over my 30+ years working with IBM i security. I decided to write this new book rather than update *IBM i Security Administration and Compliance* because I wanted an easy-to-read, focused publication describing the how-to challenges of dealing with IBM i security. Very specifically, how to work with and manage IBM i security using the newest interfaces and technologies that IBM has provided us—that is, IBM i Services, New Navigator for i, IBM i Access Client Solutions (ACS), and Authority Collection. I also wanted to provide written instructions for the techniques that I've used with my clients throughout my career to solve various security problems. Because IBM has changed values for some of the most critical security-related system values, I felt it was time for me to provide the knowledge I have to make it easier for everyone to increase the security posture of their IBM i systems without fear of breaking something… and to know how to fix things if something does break.

I'm so proud to have been associated with IBM i (formerly AS/400 and iSeries) all these years. But remember, it's *securable,* a term I coined as the Security Team Leader in Rochester, Minnesota, when reviewing IBM's marketing material for the system (iSeries at the time). I was constantly having to correct the word *secure* to *securable*…but I digress. While IBM has made some important changes in IBM i 7.5, one must still *choose* to use the features IBM has provided to have a secure system. Realizing that not everyone eats, breathes, and sleeps IBM i security like I do, I thought it would be helpful to do a "brain dump" and document my tips and techniques. If you get one thing out of this book that helps make securing your system easier or allows you to take steps to make your system more secure, I will have accomplished my goal.

You'll notice that I'm not explaining security concepts in this book. That's the purpose of my companion book, *IBM i Security Administration and Compliance, Third Edition,* so please refer to that book if that's the type of information you're looking for. Also, my goal is to help you use the latest technologies and interfaces, so my examples will focus on using New Nav, ACS, and IBM i Services. I may have to throw in a CL command or two, but I want you to modernize how you manage your security so you can take advantage of all the new features IBM's providing. You can't do that if you stay stuck in the world of CL and "green-screen."

Contents

CHAPTER 1

Technology Overview

Before we get into examples of using these technologies, I want to make sure you know how to access them as well as provide some tips for using them.

IBM i Access Client Solutions

Access Client Solutions (ACS) is the client software IBM provides for us to access IBM i. I am shocked when I repeatedly see IBM i shops continuing to use the ancient Client Access for Windows software. You *must* migrate to ACS if you haven't already done so! It's only a matter of time before Microsoft issues a patch that breaks the software or there's a new security vulnerability identified that affects the product. Because IBM no longer supports it, you'll then be scrambling to migrate your users to ACS. Do you really want to be explaining to your management why you're running software that hasn't been supported in literally years and are now panicking when you could have had a controlled rollout of the currently supported product? And just because you're running ACS doesn't mean you shouldn't pay attention to IBM Security Bulletins. Older versions of ACS have been identified as being exposed to the log4j vulnerability. In other words, you need to stay current! OK, I'll get down off my soapbox now and explain some features of ACS.

While I use many of the ACS features, the main feature I'll be using throughout this book is Run SQL Scripts. See Figure 1.1.

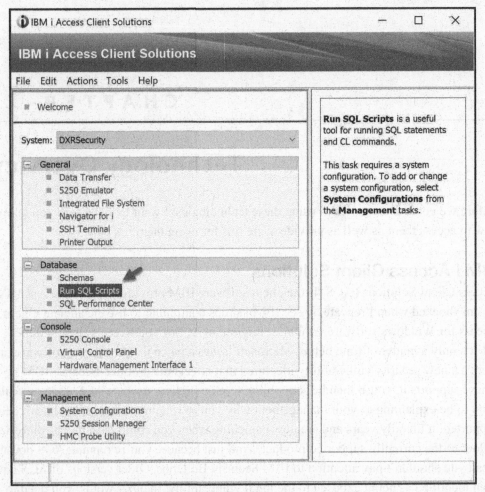

Figure 1.1: Run SQL Scripts in Access Client Solutions.

Launching Run SQL Scripts opens a window that allows you to run SQL that you write as well as take advantage of the SQL examples IBM provides and–bonus!–save your work so you don't have to re-create the SQL every time you want to run it.

First, let's see how you can take advantage of the shipped examples. After launching Run SQL Scripts, go to the toolbar and choose Edit > Examples > Insert from Examples. Using the dropdown list, choose IBM i Services. I've scrolled down to the Security section of the list. Clicking on the name of the service produces an SQL example in the right window as shown in Figure 1.2.

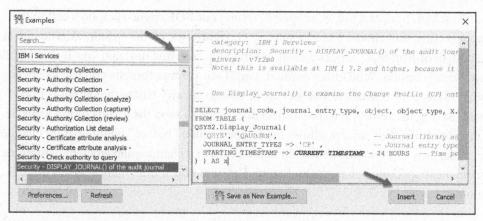

Figure 1.2: Use Insert to add the SQL example to your Run SQL Scripts window.

I learned how to write SQL by first using these examples. I found an example that was close to what I wanted, clicked on the Insert button to add it to my Run SQL Scripts window, and either ran it as is or, more often, modified it to meet my needs. I encourage you to check out these examples, especially if you're an SQL novice.

The second feature I want to point out in Run SQL Scripts is the ability to save your work. I know that, as an administrator, you don't have time to re-create your SQL every time you want to use it. To save your work, click on File in the toolbar, then Save As > PC File. You can save the file on your PC or on a common server so your teammates can also access the file. To use the saved file, click on File > Open > PC File. I use this feature ALL.THE.TIME. I have one saved for each presentation in which I'm using SQL examples, I've created files for clients and then sent the file to the client for their use, I have another file that I use when investigating new features but don't want to start from scratch, and so on. In fact, I have saved the SQL examples used throughout this book and you can download and use them yourself!

Finally, many times the results of running the SQL statement need further review or analysis. When this happens, I send the results to a spreadsheet. Here are the directions to accomplish this. Depending on the version of ACS, you'll either choose Options from the toolbar and then Enable Save Results… > For This Session. Rerun your SQL, click on a cell in the output section, right-click, and choose Save Results. Or for more recent versions of ACS, choose Edit > Preferences. Then, on the General tab, check the box labeled Enable Saving of Results and click OK. In this case, you'll have to close down your Run SQL Scripts window, reopen it, rerun your SQL, right-click on a cell in the output section, and choose Save Results.... Or right-click on the Results tab (the tab at the bottom of Run SQL Scripts that shows the SQL that was run) and you'll also get the Save Results option. With either method, you'll see various formats you can save your output to (.txt, .csv, .xlsx, etc.) as well as be able to specify where the output is to be saved. Saving the results to a spreadsheet allows me to send the results of my analysis to my clients for their review, allows me to document a "before" picture before changes are made, provides documentation for submission to a change-management committee to document upcoming changes, and more. I'm sure you'll find many ways to use this feature!

New Navigator for i

Next, the new Navigator for i browser-based interface. "New Nav" as it's fondly referred to first became available in Technology Refreshes (TRs) IBM i 7.3 TR11 and IBM i 7.4 TR5. At that time, it wasn't the default, and you had to access it using the URL http://your-system-name:2002/Navigator/login. But as of IBM i 7.5 and IBM i 7.3 TR12 and IBM i 7.4 TR6, New Nav has officially replaced Heritage Nav (the politically correct term for the old, and quite frankly ugly, previous Navigator for i interface). Now, using the URL http://your-system-name:2001 or clicking on the Navigator for i feature in Access Client Solutions (ACS) will launch New Nav.

One of my goals is to show you how to take advantage of this new and improved interface. If you happen to be on a system that is still using Heritage Nav, I encourage you to upgrade as soon as possible, not only to take advantage of the examples I'm going to show you but also to distance yourself from any vulnerabilities that may be identified in the future but not fixed (since Heritage Nav is no longer supported by IBM). To keep up to date with information regarding New Nav, see https://www.ibm.com/support/pages/node/6483299.

IBM i Services

I'll be using IBM i Services extensively in this book, so I suggest that you bookmark a couple of websites. One is the support page that lists all of the services that are available as well as the release/Technology Refresh in which they were introduced: https://www.ibm.com/support/pages/node/1119123

Services are categorized by the area of the system to which they pertain—for example, Journal Services, PTF Services, Security Services, etc. (Hint: Sometimes I find it easier to find the service I'm looking for by searching the webpage using a specific term rather than attempting to find the service in its category.) If you click on the name of a service, you may be taken to an intermediate page that lists any updates to the service along with a link to its IBM Information Center page. If no updates, you'll be taken directly to the service's page on the IBM Information Center, which details the purpose of the service, the output that will be generated, and, at the very bottom of the page, an example of using the service. An added benefit: if you want to use the SQL example they've provided, you can easily click on the icon in the upper right corner of the box containing the example to add the SQL to your clipboard!

New and enhanced services are being provided with each new version of IBM i but also with most, if not all TRs. Here's one website that helps me keep track of the enhancements: https://www.ibm.com/support/pages/node/1116645/

Authority Collection

Several of my examples will show how to use Authority Collection. Authority Collection for user profiles was introduced in IBM i 7.3 and enhanced to provide collection of individual objects in both libraries and directories in IBM i 7.4. If you're unfamiliar with the concept and configuration of the Authority Collection feature, I suggest that you read Chapter 16 in my book *IBM i Security Administration and Compliance, Third Edition* for details.

IBM i Audit Journal

Since the introduction of Authority Collection, I don't use the audit journal as much as I used to, but it remains a vital tool for investigating and solving security issues. I'll be showing numerous examples of its use throughout this book. Again, if you are unfamiliar with the basic concepts of the IBM i audit journal, please see Chapter 15 in *IBM i Security Administration and Compliance, Third Edition*. I will be using both the Copy Audit Journal Entry (CPYAUDJRNE) command, which I describe extensively in my book, as well as the IBM i audit journal table functions that allow me to bypass gathering the information into an outfile and allow me to use SQL to get information directly out of the audit journal.

I prefer using the table functions for a couple of reasons. First, I may be looking for entries for only one specific user or object, but when using CPYAUDJRNE I first must gather *all* entries of that type. The other reason I prefer using the SQL table functions is that timestamp arithmetic is *so* easy using SQL. You'll understand what I mean when you see the examples I provide. It's likely I would switch and never use CPYAUDJRNE again, but IBM hasn't yet provided the SQL table functions for all audit journal entry types. You can keep track of which audit journal types are supported at the following link (simply substitute the 7.5 for the 7.X version you're running): https://www.ibm.com/docs/en/i/7.5?topic=services-audit-journal-entry. Check this after each TR as this is not a static list! IBM has provided most of these table functions via TRs.

Finally, New Nav has added the ability to examine the audit journal. If you're new to the audit journal, or even if you're not, this is an easy way to examine audit journal entries without having to know one iota of SQL! In this book, I'll show examples of using New Nav to examine the audit journal.

CHAPTER **2**

System Values

If you've ever heard me speak on the Fundamentals of IBM i Security, you've heard me describe its three core aspects: system values, user profiles, and object security. It seems only appropriate then that the first part of this book describes how to modernize monitoring and managing these three core aspects, starting with system values.

I'm starting with a discussion of accessing and managing the security-relevant system values because they set the tone of security on IBM i. In addition, two of the most important system values have major changes in IBM i 7.5. Let's start with those changes.

Tech Note

As of IBM i 7.5, you can no longer set QSECURITY to level 20.

QSECURITY

The QSECURITY system value sets the level of security on the system. There used to be five values that you could specify for QSECURITY: 10, 20, 30, 40, and 50. But when I was still leader of the IBM i (AS/400 at the time) security team, we removed the ability to specify security level 10. Upgrading the system would not change the value, and you could restore your system values and get to level 10, but you could not change it if it somehow got set to something other than 10. As of IBM i 7.5, level 20 is no longer available. Again, you can upgrade your system and stay at level 20; however, if you restore IBM i to a system in which the original value is something other than 20, attempting to restore the QSECURITY system value set to 20 will fail. The system will set QSECURITY to whatever the original value was.

I applaud IBM for removing this value. It's truly irresponsible for any organization to be running at a level where all profiles are created with *ALLOBJ special authority! That said, I know that some organizations are still running at security level 20 (more than people realize, I believe). I'm hoping this change by IBM will cause these organizations to get a project in place to make this change. To aid in that process, I'm providing specific guidance on the process I've used to move organizations from security level 20 to 40 (as well as 30 to 40). For guidance and tips, see chapter 3, Moving to a Higher Security Level, and chapter 9, Successfully Securing Files Using Authority Collection, IBM i Services, and Auditing.

Tech Note

IBM i 7.5 adds QPWDLVL 4.

The second major change in IBM i 7.5 is to the QPWDLVL system value. A new password level (level 4) has been added, and the old LANMAN password, which was the one differentiator between password levels 0 and 1, has been removed from the system entirely (it has never been stored on levels 1 and 3). IBM i 7.5 removes it from levels 0 and 2. both level 0 and 2. The LANMAN password was used only when connecting to IBM i via a file share from a client running Windows 95, 98, or ME or Windows 2000 Server. Since none of those operating systems are supported (and haven't been for ages), IBM has taken the step to remove the storage of that old and vulnerable password. Therefore, there is no longer a difference between password level 0 and 1. Unlike the change to QSECURITY, you can still set QPWDLVL to a lower level. If your organization isn't already at level 3, I encourage you to make that move. Then, after upgrading to IBM i 7.5, make the move to password level 4. I provide guidance for moving to a higher password level in chapter 4, Moving to a Higher Password Level.

Now let's take a look at how you can access your security-relevant system value settings. Of course, there's the tried-and-true Work with System Value (WRKSYSVAL) command.

In fact, you can narrow down what's displayed by running the following to see only the security-related system values:

```
WRKSYSVAL *SEC
```

But what if you want to use New Navigator for i or SQL? In the section below called New Nav: System Values, we'll look at New Nav. But first, let's take a look at the two options SQL provides.

```
QSYS2.SYSTEM_VALUE_INFO
```

Run without any qualifying WHERE clause, this service lists all system values along with their current value. You can modify it to list all of the password system values since they all begin with 'QPWD' like this:

```
SELECT *
    FROM QSYS2.SYSTEM_VALUE_INFO
    WHERE system_value_name LIKE 'QPWD%';
```

But there's no easy way to list just the security-related system values like there is with WRKSYSVAL. For this reason, I find this service to be of limited use. However, I think you'll find this next service quite useful.

QSYS2.SECURITY_INFO

This service is similar to running the Display Security Attributes (DSPSECA) and Display Security Auditing (DSPSECAUD) CL commands along with the Retrieve Security Attributes API (QSYRTVSA). But instead of calling two CL commands that only go to display or write to an API, you can retrieve all security-related values (including security-relevant system values) in one easy select statement!

If you've ever run DSPSECA, you know that it displays somewhat random security configuration information, but if you need that information, it's the only place you can discover it. For example, I find it useful to run DSPSECA to determine if a change to either QSECURITY or QPWDLVL has taken effect or is still pending. DSPSECA shows both the current and pending values. (Remember, it takes an IPL for changes to these system values to take effect.) Note: If the current and pending values are the same, only the current value is displayed. And I find running DSPSECAUD helpful to determine which audit journal receiver is currently attached. For more information about QSYS2. SECURITY_INFO, see https://www.ibm.com/support/pages/node/6442035

While this information is valuable, the format of the information returned is not that easy to consume. All of the information is returned on one line. You must endlessly scroll to the right of your Run SQL Scripts display to see all of them. Enter New Nav. What you're going to realize once you've used IBM i Services and New Nav a few times is that they are very tightly connected. New Nav uses IBM i Services to present most of its information. Let's see how New Nav displays this information.

New Nav: Security Information

To see the information provided by the QSYS2.SECURITY_INFO service in New Nav, log into New Nav, float your cursor over the padlock, and click on Security Configuration Info, as shown in Figure 2.1.

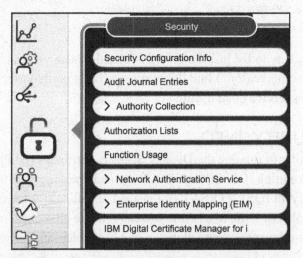

Figure 2.1: Click on the padlock icon and then Security Configuration Info to see the listing of security information, current and pending settings, and a description of the value.

What's displayed is an aggregation of the system values returned when running WRKSYSVAL *SEC, the security attributes displayed when running DSPSECA, and the audit configuration settings displayed when running DSPSECAUD. A description of each system value, attribute, or configuration setting is provided, along with its list of possible values. One thing I appreciate about this view is that each possible value is explained, as shown in Figure 2.2. Under the covers, New Nav has called the QSYS2.SECURITY_ INFO IBM i Service but is displaying it in a much more consumable format than if you'd run the service in Run SQL Scripts.

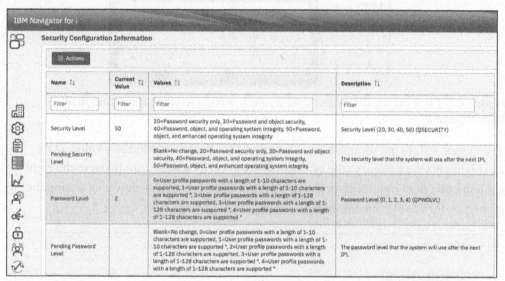

Figure 2.2: An example of two values shown under the Security Configuration Info category.

I find this view quite helpful, and I think you will too, especially if you don't work with IBM i security very often or you're new to the topic.

New Nav: System Values

You can also get a listing of all system values, including the security-relevant system values, in New Nav. To access these values, float your cursor over what, to me, looks like a clipboard. See Figure 2.3.

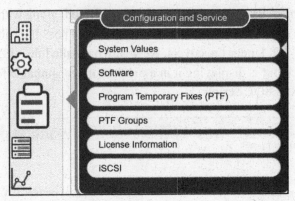

Figure 2.3: Click on the clipboard then System Values to view and manage all system values.

The system values are grouped into categories. To display or change a value, click on (highlight) the category (the system values in each category are listed in the right column), and then right-click and choose Properties. Figure 2.4 shows an example of the properties for the Signon category.

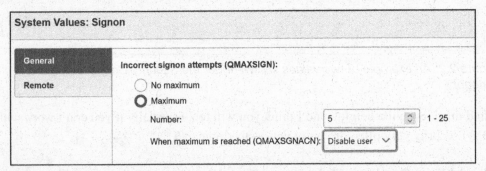

Figure 2.4: Click on the Signon category to display/change the signon-related system values.

If you need a description of each security-relevant system value or recommendations for best-practice settings, see chapter 3 of *IBM i Security Administration and Compliance, Third Edition*.

Using the Audit Journal to Detect System Value Changes

I have many clients that require regular review of system value changes. The best way to do that is to review the changes using the SV audit journal entries. While you can use the method that's been around for many, many releases (Copy Audit Journal Entry (CPYAUDJRNE)) and then run a query on the resulting file QTEMP/QAUDITSV, I prefer to use the method IBM is now providing for us: a one-step method to pull the entries out of the audit journal.

The following will produce a list of system value changes made in the last two weeks, omitting the changes made via the QNTC server.

```
SELECT entry_timestamp,
     user_name,
     system_value,
     new_value,
     old_value
  FROM TABLE (
         systools.audit_journal_sv(STARTING_TIMESTAMP => CURRENT
            TIMESTAMP - 14 DAYS)
     )
  WHERE system_value <> 'ADJUTC';
```

CHAPTER 3

Moving to a Higher Security Level

I can't believe I'm still talking about this topic after all these years, but alas, there are still many organizations whose system is not running at the recommended value of QSECURITY level 40 (or 50.) This chapter has two sections—one specific to moving from QSECURITY level 30 to level 40 and the other dedicated to moving from QSECURITY level 20 to 40. Regardless of whether the system is at 20 or 30, you must determine whether any programs on the system are violating the rules of level 40, so that's where I'm going to start.

Moving from QSECURITY Level 30 to 40

At security level 40, the operating system prevents certain actions from being taken. Examples include calling an operating system program directly, accessing an internal control block, and using a job description that names a user profile in which the caller doesn't have authority to the named profile. The good news is that, while not prevented at security level 20 or 30, these actions are logged into the audit journal as AF (authority failure) entries. This allows us to determine whether there are any issues prior to going to level 40. If you like to live on the wild side, you can most certainly move QSECURITY to 40 and IPL without doing any investigation! But should you run into issues, it's a hard stop. In other words, your program will fail with a function check, and there's no getting around the error. You must fix it to continue—that, or IPL back to level 30. I prefer to be a bit more cautious, especially when it comes to production systems, so I always check the audit journal prior to the IPL.

Audit to Determine Whether There Are Issues Prior to Moving to Level 40

Determining whether there are issues that need to be resolved prior to going to level 40 is quite easy. It's a matter of adding *AUTFAIL and *PGMFAIL to the QAUDLVL system value and making sure *AUDLVL has been specified in QAUDCTL. Then it's simply a matter of looking for AF audit journal entries. But not all AF entries. Believe it or not, we don't care if there are AF subtype A entries. Those failures indicate someone didn't have authority to an object. Nor do we care about AF subtype K entries. Those failures indicate the profile attempting an action didn't have the required special authority. For this investigation, we are only interested in the subtypes that are specific to level 40. (The subtype is the first character of the entry-specific part of the AF audit journal entry.) The subtypes we need to look for are C, D, J, R, and S. All of these indicate actions that will cause a failure at level 40.

Examining the audit journal for these entries isn't hard. If you're using Copy Audit Journal Entries (CPYAUDJRNE), your commands will look like this:

```
CPYAUDJRNE ENTTYP(AF) JRNRCV(*CURCHAIN)
STRSQL
SELECT AFTSTP, AFJOB, AFUSER, AFNBR, AFPGM, AFPGMLIB, AFUSPF,
AFVIOL, AFONAM, AFOLIB, AFOTYP, AFINST FROM qtemp/qauditaf WHERE
AFVIOL in ('C','D','J','R','S');
```

But I prefer a more modern approach. AF is one of the types provided as an SQL table function, so I recommend that you open up ACS, click on Run SQL Scripts, and run this:

```
SELECT entry_timestamp,
       user_name,
       qualified_job_name,
       program_library,
       program_name,
       violation_type,
       violation_type_detail,
       object_library,
       object_name,
       object_type,
       program_instruction
```

```
FROM TABLE (
         systools.audit_journal_af()
     )
WHERE violation_type IN ('C', 'D', 'J', 'R', 'S');
```

Note that I've included two fields that are not available when using the CPYAUDJRNE method: qualified_job_name and violation_type_detail. I find the latter to be very useful when explaining these entries to my clients. I think you'll find them useful too. See Figure 3.1.

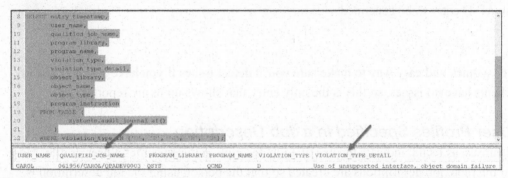

Figure 3.1: Some fields are available using the SQL table but not CPYAUDJRNE.

Domain Failures

The entries I typically find at my clients are D (domain failures) and more often, J (job description use). If you have any domain failures, the program name and library in the D audit journal entry identify the program running at the time of the failure. The object name is the object being accessed, and if there's an instruction number, that's the statement number in the program where the object is accessed. It's usually that an operating system program is being called rather than a command or API. One of my clients had domain failures because they were directly calling the program that's called by the SIGNOFF command rather than calling the command itself. Why the original programmer coded it this way is beyond me, but it was an easy fix, as most domain failures are.

I have not seen an application that doesn't run at QSECURITY level 40 for many, many years. However, you may see some AF-D entries listed for them. Some vendors still take a different code path at the lower security levels than at level 40 or 50. If you discover entries for vendor products, don't assume there's an issue. A quick call to the vendor will verify that their application does run at level 40 and you can ignore those audit journal entries.

I will often find no audit journal entries and wonder whether my SQL is correct or I'm missing something. If I need to test my method, I'll force an AF-D entry. That's easily done by attempting to call an operating system program. Since I'm familiar with it, I attempt to directly call the program that's called by the Create User Profile (CRTUSRPRF) command. Simply running the following from a command line will cause an AF-D entry to be generated:

```
CALL QSYUP
```

It's a quick and easy way to make sure you'll detect issues if you have any. Most of my clients have no issues, so this is the only entry that shows up in my reports.

User Profiles Specified in a Job Description

J entries, as I said, indicate the use of a job description that specifies a user profile. Most of the time, job descriptions are created so that the person using the job description is the profile under which the job runs. But the USER parameter can be specified with the name of a user profile. In this case, when the job description is used, the job runs as the profile specified in the USER parameter. The problem with this and the exposure it causes at QSECURITY levels 20 and 30 is that, at these levels, the user only needs authority to the job description, not the user profile named in the job description. Therefore, if you have a job description that names a powerful profile, people can use the job description and elevate their authority. Vendors will often ship job descriptions that name powerful profiles (that is, profiles that have all special authorities) with their products. If those job descriptions are not *PUBLIC *EXCLUDE, they're an exposure if your system's not at QSECURITY level 40 or 50. (At levels 40 and 50, attempting to use a job description that names a user profile to which you don't have *USE authority will fail.) But it's not just vendors that do this. I've also seen client-created job descriptions that specify a profile.

So what do you do if you encounter J entries? Part of your challenge will be to determine which job description caused the audit entry. One would think that would be in the audit journal entry, but it's not. What's listed is the user profile named in the job description. The easiest way to get the list of job descriptions that specify the user profile in the AF-J entry is to use the QSYS2.JOB_DESCRIPTION IBM i Service as follows (obviously substituting the profile named in the audit journal entry for XXXX).

```
SELECT job_description_library,
       job_description,
       authorization_name
    FROM QSYS2.JOB_DESCRIPTION_INFO
    WHERE authorization_name = 'XXXX';
```

If it's not obvious which job description is causing the issue (often looking at the job description's last used date will make it obvious), you can start Authority Collection on the job descriptions to determine who and which processes are using them. But I've never had to go to that length to figure it out.

What do you do once you've identified the offending job descriptions? I've found that, in most cases, either the job description no longer has to be used or it's preferred that the job run as the actual user, so the USER parameter is changed back to the default of *RQD or it's switched out to another job description. The absolute last resort that I use to resolve this issue is to set the profile to *PUBLIC *USE. It's the last resort because it allows the profile to be specified, not just in job descriptions but also on a Submit Job (SBMJOB) command. And I would take this step only if the profile had no special authorities and did not own the application (or anything else important).

I have not seen an application or system that cannot be moved to QSECURITY level 40 (or 50) in ages. Most of my clients have had no changes to make and can IPL to level 40 without issue. Obviously, you'll want to audit to make sure that's the case for you, but even if you discover something that needs to be changed, it's unlikely that it will be a major change.

Moving from QSECURITY Level 20 to 40

 Tech Note

As of IBM i 7.5, you cannot change QSECURITY to run at level 20.

I have to be honest. Moving from QSECURITY level 20 to 40 is a much different story than the 30 to 40 move. Simply put, the move is not trivial. But because QSECURITY level 20 will no longer be an option as of IBM i 7.5 and I know there are still systems running at this security level, I'm going to describe how I've helped organizations make this move.

The only difference between QSECURITY level 20 and 30 is that at level 20 *all* profiles are created—by default—with *ALLOBJ, *SAVSYS, and *JOBCTL special authorities. When you IPL the system off of level 20 to anything higher, the system adjusts the users' special authorities based on the value of the User Class (*USRCLS) parameter in the user profile. This is the absolute *only* time you'll ever hear me talking about the importance of the user class setting, but in this one scenario, it's critical.

The primary reason it's so difficult to move off of level 20 is because at level 20 you basically don't have to worry about security at all because all profiles have *ALLOBJ. So now you're moving from an environment where security isn't a concern to one where it is. Of course, this is the perfect opportunity to rework your application security design to be more secure, possibly even implementing a deny-by-default approach. But even if you don't want to go to those lengths, you can't ignore the fact that *ALLOBJ is going to be removed from most users, and if your application's *PUBLIC authority settings aren't set to accommodate all actions being taken, there will be authority failures. While there's no way to use the audit journal to know what will fail (as you can with the 30 to 40 move), the good news is that the same authority-checking algorithm runs at all security levels. This means that you can remove some users' *ALLOBJ special authority while still running at security level 20 to test your application and make the necessary adjustments prior to IPLing. You can also—and I encourage you to—audit for security level 40 issues at the same time. It's a waste of time to IPL from 20 to 30 and then audit for level 40 issues and then IPL to 40. You can easily make the move from 20 directly to 40.

Analyzing and Adjusting Profiles' User Class
The analysis for moving off of QSECURITY 20 begins with analyzing the profiles' user class settings. To get this listing, we'll make use of the QSYS2.USER_INFO IBM i Service:

```
SELECT authorization_name,
       user_class_name,
```

```
      special_authorities,
      text_description
  FROM qsys2.user_info
  ORDER BY user_class_name;
```

I've included the currently assigned special authorities in my SQL so you can see what special authorities may potentially be stripped away when you IPL. I say "potentially" because the special authorities will be assigned based on the user's user class, as shown in Table 3.1 from chapter 2 of the *IBM i Security Reference* manual.

Table 2. Default special authorities for user classes by security level					
Special authority	**User classes**				
	*SECOFR	***SECADM**	***PGMR**	***SYSOPR**	***USER**
*ALLOBJ	All	10 or 20	10 or 20	10 or 20	10 or 20
*AUDIT	All				
*IOSYSCFG	All				
*JOBCTL	All	10 or 20	10 or 20	All	
*SAVSYS	All	10 or 20	10 or 20	All	10 or 20
*SECADM	All	All			
*SERVICE	All				
*SPLCTL	All				

Table 3.1: Table from chapter 2 of the IBM i Security Reference *manual shows special assignments by user class.*

I encourage you to assign users to a user class that best matches their job responsibilities. Special authorities may have been assigned throughout the years but may no longer be (or never were) necessary. Now is the perfect time to reduce excess special authorities. This means that most profiles should be assigned to the *USER user class.

Obviously, security and system administrators will likely be assigned to the *SECOFR user class. But you may have some service accounts that are designed to have *ALLOBJ special authority—perhaps a profile designated to run all job scheduler jobs. What do you do with this profile's user class? You have two choices: leave it in the *USER user class and assign *ALLOBJ once the IPL has taken place or assign it to the *SECOFR user class. I prefer the former. It's unlikely that any service account needs all special authorities. Assigning it to the *SECOFR user class may be convenient, but you risk leaving that profile with way more special authorities than are required. It's likely that you're going to have a list of profiles that need adjusting after the IPL, so add these service accounts to that list.

Another set of profiles you may need to adjust are your programmers—or at least the profile your programmers use to debug production issues. It's likely that profile will need *JOBCTL special authority after the IPL has taken place. In this case, I'd assign the special authorities required to their group. Or, if they don't belong to a group, take this opportunity to create a group for them and assign it *JOBCTL so you only have one profile to adjust after the IPL.

Determine the Users' Source of Authority to Application Data after IPLing

The next step is to determine how users are going to have sufficient authority to run the application once their *ALLOBJ authority has been removed. You must first decide what your security posture is going to be after the IPL. Do you want to have a secure posture so data can only be accessed by those with a business requirement—in other words, deny by default? Do you want to make sure the integrity of the data is in place but allow all people with a user profile to read it? Perhaps you have a handful of files containing confidential data that must be secured and the rest are not of concern (or you only have time to focus on those confidential files right now). Or do you know that you need to get your system off of level 20 and just want to do the bare minimum to accomplish that? Of course, I can't dictate which posture you choose, but obviously my preference would be to have a deny-by-default approach to securing your data.

I've provided examples of listing object authorities and ownership in chapter 7, so look at those. Also, for a detailed explanation of implementing object-level security for an application, see chapter 17 in *IBM i Security Administration and Compliance, Third Edition*.

Here are the high-level steps you must take for each approach:

- Implementing a deny-by-default approach is most labor-intensive. You must identify the libraries that contain the data to be secured (I omit the libraries associated with vendor tools that don't actually contain data—for example, job schedulers), determine which profile will own the application, ensure all application objects are owned by this profile, set program objects to adopt this owner's authority, and secure physical and logical files with an authorization list. That's the setup. The analysis is the intensive portion because you must identify any profile that's updating or reading application files using an interface such as via ODBC or FTP—that is, not using an application program to read or update the file. Profiles accessing the data using non-application programs must be authorized to the authorization list securing the file. Again, step-by-step instructions for this approach are in my companion book.

- Implementing a data-integrity approach—that is, ensuring the data can be updated only via the application but can be read by all—requires the same setup as the deny-by-default approach. What makes this much less work is that you have to detect only the profiles that are legitimately changing the data outside of the application because, instead of setting the *PUBLIC authority of the database files to *EXCLUDE as you do in the deny-by-default model, you set the *PUBLIC authority to *USE. Therefore, the number of audit journal entries you have to analyze is significantly less. That said, if you have confidential data or Personally Identifiable Information (PII), this approach is not sufficient to protect that data. In this case, you need to go for either the full deny-by-default approach or a hybrid approach that secures some files more strictly than others. If you can identify where your confidential data resides, you can use Authority Collection to see which profiles are accessing it. Authority Collection is a great tool, but it generates so much information that it's difficult to use to secure all files in an application. However, it's fantastic when the focus is a handful of files. You'll see examples of using Authority Collection in chapters 6 and 9.

- If you are focusing only on a handful (10 or fewer) files, I recommend that you use Authority Collection to determine who is accessing those files and by which interface. If access is via an application program, you can set the program to adopt authority as long as the owner of the program also owns (or is authorized) to the file. If access is via an interface such as ODBC or query or SSH, then you may want to consider attaching an authorization list, setting the file's *PUBLIC to *AUTL, and setting the *PUBLIC authority of the authorization list to *EXCLUDE. Then authorize the users requiring access as identified via the file's Authority Collection entries.

Using one of these two methods will take care of the files containing confidential information. But what about the rest of the application objects? How will users have sufficient authority to those once *ALLOBJ is removed from their profile? It's highly likely that the current *PUBLIC authority setting of the rest of the application objects will be sufficient. That's because, when creating most objects, the object's *PUBLIC authority is set based on the value of the QCRTAUT system value. IBM ships this system value as *CHANGE. Therefore, most application objects are likely set to *PUBLIC *CHANGE. *CHANGE authority will be (more than) sufficient for most operations performed by the application. The only issue you may have is with database files. Specifically, if the application is doing something such as adding a physical file member or creating a duplicate copy of an application file, then *CHANGE won't be sufficient. This underscores the importance of implementing and testing your new security scheme at QSECURITY level 20 prior to IPLing and having all users' authorities adjusted.

- Now for the two approaches you can take if you just want to get off level 20:

  ○ Determine which profiles own the applications your users are running and assign each owner as a group profile for the application users. I absolutely do not like this approach because it gives those users *ALL authority to the application objects, including the data. (The owner of an object has *ALL authority, and everything a group owns, all members own.) However, it's better than users having *ALLOBJ, which is the second choice.

  ○ Last and very much least and one I absolutely don't recommend: After IPLing to level 40, grant back *ALLOBJ to every user. The *only* good thing about this approach is that level 40 provides operating system integrity, which cannot be achieved below level 40.

If you want to understand the gory details of the differences between each security level, see chapter 3 in *IBM i Security Administration and Compliance, Third Edition* or chapter 2 in the *IBM i Security Reference* manual.

CHAPTER 4

Moving to a Higher Password Level

The system value QPWDLVL controls the password formats stored as well as the length and character set available for users' passwords. Changes to this system value take effect with the next IPL. Because IBM is making changes to this system value in IBM i 7.5, it's time to re-examine what it takes to move to a higher level and hopefully get all systems to at least level 3. I'll discuss this system value in three sets: Password levels 0 and 1, password levels 2 and 3, and password level 4 (introduced in IBM i 7.5).

QPWDLVLs 0 and 1

Password levels 0 and 1 define that a user's password will have a maximum length of 10 characters and can consist only of uppercase A–Z, numerals 0–9, and special characters #, @, $, and _. The problem with these two levels is the restricted character set. The small number of possibilities of password combinations means that passwords are relatively easy to guess and can certainly be brute-force attacked in a short period of time. The difference between the various password levels is the format of the passwords stored. But as I say that, let me clarify.

The actual password is never stored in IBM i. In fact, as the *IBM i Security Reference* manual explains, the password is actually part of the key used in the encryption algorithm for what is stored. Also, it's a one-way algorithm, so the value is never decrypted to get back to the cleartext password. Rather, the value that's provided as the password when presented along with the profile for authentication goes through the same algorithm, and the encrypted values are compared. If they're the same, the user is authenticated and the user is signed on or the connection is established. So while in this chapter I refer to the "versions of the passwords" that are stored, please understand that that's not literal. It's just that I believe the concepts are easier to understand using that terminology.

At password level 0, one of the formats stored is a very weakly encrypted version that's used when users are connecting to the NetServer. This version is known to be vulnerable, so no one should want to keep it around. The good news, however, is that the only connections using this password are those coming from computers running Windows 95, 98, or ME or Windows 2000 Server and connecting to the NetServer via a file share. Please tell me that your organization is not running one of these ancient operating systems! Or if you are, I can't believe it's connecting to IBM i via a file share; therefore, for the vast majority of you, you'll be able to move to password level 1 (that is, set QPWDLVL to 1 and IPL) and experience absolutely no issues. In fact, because these operating systems are so far out of support, IBM has taken the action to no longer store this weak password beginning in IBM i 7.5. If your system is not yet at 7.5 and it's still at QPWDLVL 0, I highly recommend that you at least move to level 1 to remove the weakly encrypted Microsoft password.

Tech Note

As of IBM i 7.5, IBM is no longer storing the weakly encrypted Microsoft password at any password level.

The Benefits of Moving to QPWDLVL 2 Then 3

What I'd prefer, however, is that you consider moving to an even higher level, with password level 4 being your ultimate goal. First, the benefits of moving to password level 2 or 3:

- Moving the system to one of these levels enables passwords that can be up to 128 characters and can contain any value—uppercase and lowercase letters, numerals, punctuation, spaces, and any special characters. This increases the password character set tremendously and reduces the chances of having the password guessed (assuming appropriate composition rules are applied) and increases the time required to perform a brute-force attack.

- If you need to, you can keep the maximum length of a password at 10, but even by doing that, because of the greatly increased character set that the password can contain, you've made it much harder for people to guess a password.

- Password level 2 or 3 also makes the QPWDRULES system value more usable. When using QPWDRULES, you put all of your password composition rules in this one system value (min length, max length, etc. rather than using the individual QPWDMINLEN, for example). Then, I suggest you add the value of *REQANY3 - *require any 3*, so now users must specify three of the following four in their password: an uppercase letter, a lowercase letter, a digit, or a special character.

- Password level 2 or 3 usually makes it easier for the IBM i passwords to have the same requirements as the network password.

- Users will *not* have to change their password right away unless you force them to. They can use their existing password even after the system moves to password level 2 or 3.

Changes That Occur with QPWDLVL 2 or 3

Setting changes to QPWDLVL requires an IPL. Here are the changes you'll see after the IPL to level 2 or 3 from 0 or 1.

- The password field on the sign-on screen now accommodates a password of up to 128 characters. See Figure 4.1. If you've modified the sign-on display that ships with the system, you'll now have to modify the DDS (the display specifications) that includes the 128-character password field. See chapter 6 in the *IBM i Security Reference* manual for instructions.

```
                            Sign On
                                      System  . . . . . :   DXREX74
                                      Subsystem . . . . . :   QINTER
                                      Display . . . . . . :   QPADEV0003

        User   . . . . . . . . . . . . . . .     _____
        Password . . . . . . . . . . . . . .     _____

                                                      _
        Program/procedure . . . . . . . .        _____
        Menu   . . . . . . . . . . . . . .        _____
        Current library . . . . . . . . .        _____
```

Figure 4.1: The sign-on display after IPLing to QPWDLVL 2 or 3. Notice the increased length of the Password field.

- Prompts for the CRTUSRPRF and CHGUSRPRF commands are changed to allow input of up to 128 characters for the User password parameter. See Figure 4.2.

```
                        Create User Profile (CRTUSRPRF)

 Type choices, press Enter.

 User profile . . . . . . . . . .   new_prof      Name
 User password  . . . . . . . . .   This is a valid password when running QSECUR
ITY level 2 or 3 - Isn't this S0000 cool?!?!?

 Set password to expired  . . . .   *NO           *NO, *YES
 Status . . . . . . . . . . . . .   *ENABLED      *ENABLED, *DISABLED
 User class . . . . . . . . . . .   *USER         *USER, *SYSOPR, *PGMR...
 Assistance level . . . . . . . .   *SYSVAL       *SYSVAL, *BASIC, *INTERMED...
 Current library  . . . . . . . .   *CRTDFT       Name, *CRTDFT
 Initial program to call  . . . .   *NONE         Name, *NONE
   Library  . . . . . . . . . . .                 Name, *LIBL, *CURLIB
 Initial menu . . . . . . . . . .   MAIN          Name, *SIGNOFF
   Library  . . . . . . . . . . .      *LIBL      Name, *LIBL, *CURLIB
 Limit capabilities . . . . . . .   *NO           *NO, *PARTIAL, *YES
 Text 'description' . . . . . . .   *BLANK

                                                                       Bottom
 F3=Exit    F4=Prompt   F5=Refresh   F10=Additional parameters   F12=Cancel
 F13=How to use this display          F24=More keys
```

Figure 4.2: At QPWDLVL 2 or 3, the User password parameter in both the Create and Change User Profile commands is 128 characters long.

Before I discuss the considerations you'll want to make prior to moving to password level 2 or 3, I need to explain the passwords that are stored at each password level (again, not literally!). Understanding this will help ensure a successful move to a higher level.

At password levels 0 and 1, passwords are stored encrypted in two formats—one where the password is all uppercase and one where the password is all lowercase. (As I've discussed earlier, until IBM i 7.5, password level 0 had an additional format—a weakly encrypted password used to connect to the NetServer via old clients.) When the system moves to 2 or 3 and a password is provided for authentication on either a sign-on display or a connection such as FTP or ODBC, passwords are no longer "folded" to be all uppercase or lowercase. At levels 2 and 3, whatever is provided for the password—mixed case or single case—is what the system is going to use for authentication. See Table 4.1 for more details.

After the system moves to password level 2 or 3 but before the user changes their password, what continues to be stored is the all-lowercase and all-uppercase versions of the password. Either the all-lowercase or the all-uppercase password can be used for authentication. Once the password has been changed, the mixed-case password is stored, and that's what will be used for authentication. Note that at password level 2, the all-uppercase and all-lowercase passwords continue to be generated *if* the password adheres to the limits of password level 0 or 1 (maximum length 10, only special characters of #, @, $, and _, etc.).

Why should you care about this or understand how this works? You'll need to know this to understand how to guide your users after the IPL to the higher password level and to know what to look for to make sure all your connections (such as ODBC and FTP) will work after moving to the higher password level.

User Enters This Password	What's Stored at QPWDLVL 0 or 1	What's Stored at QPWDLVL 2	What's Stored at QPWDLVL 3
CarolW00d	CAROLW00D (all uppercase) carolw00d (all lowercase)	Until password is changed only: CAROLW00D (all uppercase) carolw00d (all lowercase) After password is changed, the mixed-case password is stored. The uppercase and lowercase versions are also stored as long as they meet the criteria of password level 0 or 1 (no longer than 10 characters, no special characters other than what's allowed at 0 or 1, etc.). The mixed-case version is what's used for authentication: CarolW00d (mixed case)	Until password is changed: CAROLW00D (all uppercase) carolw00d (all lowercase) After password is changed, only the mixed-case version is stored: CarolW00d (mixed case)

Table 4.1: This table shows the formats of passwords stored at each of the password levels prior to IBM i 7.5.

Here are some considerations you'll want to make along with what has the potential to break:

- End users: By far, the biggest issue you'll encounter with moving to a higher password level is going to be with your end users. That's because many users use the same password throughout the network and most networks require mixed-case passwords. So even though IBM i is running at a level that doesn't recognize mixed-case passwords, the users enter their password in mixed-case, thinking it does. (Can't blame them really. How would they know that the system is actually taking what they enter and folding it to be all lowercase or all uppercase and using that to determine whether they can sign on? They simply enter their password and it works!)

The key to success with your end users is education. Prior to IPLing, you must educate them—likely with multiple emails, Teams or Slack notifications, or whatever communications vehicles you have—to get through to them that the first time they sign on to the system after this specific system outage, they *must* use all lowercase or all uppercase (choose one format to avoid even more confusion) when they sign in to IBM i. Then, require the users to change their passwords so that the system recognizes a mixed-case password. By doing that, the point of confusion will be the first sign-on after the IPL. After they change their password, life will go back to normal.

You've probably already figured out that this will affect all users at the same time. Unfortunately, there's no way to roll this out in a staged fashion. And yes, this is going to be one hellish day for you and your help desk (you'll likely owe them treats after this). But again, the more you can educate/warn your users, the easier the days after this IPL will be.

Note that the system *does not* require the users' passwords to be changed when you IPL to a higher password level. Requiring a password change takes a conscious choice (and action) on your part.

- If you have any utilities that reset a user's password (perhaps used by your help desk, for example), you'll want to modify those to allow for the longer password. This is especially true if you choose to also change your password composition rules at the same time—for example, switching to use QPWDRULES and adding the rule *ALLCRTCHG. This means that new passwords—even when specified in CHGUSRPRF—must follow all password composition rules.

- Connections: In general, all connections should work when the hard-coded password is not currently mixed case. By this I mean connections that are made from another server to your IBM i using ODBC, JDBC, DDM, FTP, etc. These connections are typically established with a script that contains a hard-coded password for the profile being used to connect to IBM i. These connections will work unless the password currently being used is hard-coded to be in mixed case. As Table 4.1 showed, even after moving to QPWDLVL 2 or 3, the all-lowercase and all-uppercase passwords will be stored until the password is changed. What I recommend you do is find the connections (e.g., FTP, ODBC, SSH, etc.) being made to IBM i and verify that the password used is hard-coded to be either all lowercase or all uppercase. Doing that will ensure the initial connection after IPLing to the higher password level will be successful. Once you've IPLed the system, then change the hard-coded password in the script as well as the password on IBM i and take advantage of the ability to specify a more complex (that is, stronger) password for these connections.

- Replication software: If you have replication software in place and you can't move both systems to a higher password level at the same time, you'll want to make sure that you move to the higher password level on the target system before you move the source system to eliminate the possibility of creating a password on one system that isn't valid on the other.

- This same premise also applies to software that specifically replicates passwords around your network. These products are sometimes called single sign-on products, but what they're actually doing is replicating passwords. Again, you'll want to make sure to upgrade the target systems first to ensure that the initial password created will be accepted on all target systems. For example, if the originating system requires a password of 14 characters but the target system hasn't been moved to password level 2 or 3 yet, attempting to replicate the password will fail.

Note that if you have used the QSYRUPWD and QSYSUPWD APIs to securely replicate passwords between systems, the format of what's returned has changed in IBM i 7.5 and you will have to take additional steps if you need to move the password to a system running a pre-7.5 version. See the IBM i 7.5 API documentation in the IBM Information Center for details.

Moving to QPWDLVL 2 Then 3

The ultimate goal should be to get to password level 3 because password level 2 starts storing the old (and weak) Microsoft password again. You might be tempted to jump right to password level 3, but if something's not quite right and you have to move back down to level 0 or 1, it's going to be painful. If you IPL from level 3 directly back to 0 or 1, you will not be able to sign on. Trust me. It happened to me (fortunately, on a test system). To sign on, I had to have the administrator go in through DST and reset the QSECOFR user profile password. Why couldn't I sign on? Because as Table 4.1 showed, there's no password stored at password level 3 that works at level 0 or 1. To get back to password level 0 or 1, you must IPL to level 2, set your password (either via CHGUSRPF or CHGPWD) to a password that you know will be accepted at those levels (meaning the password can only use the character set allowed by password levels 0 or 1) as well as reset all of the other profiles' passwords, and then IPL back to level 0 or 1. In other words, the password that's stored at level 3 or will work only at level 2 or 3, not 0 or 1. So backing off of level 3 is really a two-step process: first go to level 2, then go to level 0 or 1. The better approach is to go to level 2 and hang there until you know all of your connections are working. Once you know all your connections work, then IPL to level 3. If you have to back down from level 2 to 0 or 1, there's a password stored that will work for each user at those levels (assuming that it's a max length of 10 and doesn't use special characters that aren't supported at level 0 or 1). For that reason, you may want to hold off requiring more-complex passwords until you know everything's working at level 2.

For systems prior to IBM i 7.5, to determine which profiles have passwords that will work at a lower password level, run the Print User Profile (PRTUSRPRF) command specifying TYPE(*PWDLVL), run Display Authorized Users (DSPAUTUSR), or run the SQL shown in Figure 4.3.

```
37  SELECT authorization_name,
38         password_level_0_1,
39         password_level_2_3,
40         text_description
41      FROM qsys2.user_info;
```

Authorization Name			Text Description
AUTHORIZATION_NAME	PASSWORD_LEVEL_0_1	PASSWORD_LEVEL_2_3	TEXT_DESCRIPTION
ACCTNG	-	-	
BOLHUI	NO	YES	Larry Bolhuis iInTheCloud
CAROL	NO	YES	Carol Woodbury

Figure 4.3: Neither the profile BOLHUI nor CAROL has a password stored that will work at password level 0 or 1.

Since my system is running at password level 3, if I needed to go back down to level 0 or 1, I would have to IPL to level 2, set the password for at least my own profile, and then IPL to 0 or 1 so that I could be assured of being able to sign on. Then, I'd have to set the password for all other profiles since the SQL above shows that no profiles have a password that will be accepted at level 0 or 1.

Up until IBM i 7.4, QPWDLVL 3 is where you want to be because, at that level, the only password that's stored is the one that works at password levels 2 and 3. You'll just want to get there in steps.

Tech Note

As of IBM i 7.5, a new password level is provided, level 4.

QPWDLVL 4

A new password level, 4, was introduced in IBM i 7.5. This password level implements an even stronger method of encrypting the password. To facilitate the move to QPWDLVL 4, as of IBM i 7.5, IBM now generates passwords at QPWDLVL 2 and 3 that will work when the system is IPLed to QPWDLVL 4. See Table 4.2 for the password variations that are stored as of IBM i 7.5.

Passwords Generated at QPWDLVL 0 or 1	Passwords Generated at QPWDLVL 2	Passwords Generated at QPWDLVL 3	Passwords Generated at QPWDLVL 4
All uppercase All lowercase	Mixed case All uppercase All lowercase Mixed case, Level 4	Mixed case Mixed case, Level 4	Level 4 version only

Table 4.2: This table shows the passwords generated and stored by password level as of IBM i 7.5.

Note that no level 4 passwords are generated when the system's at QPWDLVL 0 or 1. In other words, you need to make sure you can use longer passwords before making the move to level 4. (The system doesn't actually allow you to go from 0 or 1 directly to 4.) Also, you'll want to make sure the software you use to connect to IBM i, such as ACS and Navigator for i, have been updated. These and other client software solutions use something called "password substitution." (This is the technology used so these clients don't send passwords in cleartext when connecting to IBM i.) You'll need to make sure that this technology is current for IBM i 7.5 or later so you can be assured it's generating the password substitution values required for password level 4. To determine if profiles have a password that will work at level 4, a new password level has been added to PRTUSRPRF, DSPAUTUSR, and the qsys2.user_info service.

```
SELECT authorization_name,
       password_level_0_1,
       password_level_2_3,
       password_level_4,
       text_description
  FROM qsys2.user_info;
```

Considerations for moving to QPWDLVL 4:

- As I mentioned earlier, you'll need to make sure you're running current client software prior to moving to password level 4.

- If you need to move down from password level 4 to 0 or 1, just like moving from password level 3, you'll need to IPL to level 2, set passwords that can be used at level 0 or 1, and then IPL to the lower level.

- If you're using the QSYRUPWD or QSYSUPWD APIs to distribute passwords between systems, you'll have to have special PTFs applied to distribute the passwords from a system running password level 4 to a system running a lower level.

CHAPTER 5

User Profiles

Next up for my discussion on the foundation of IBM i security are user profiles. I realize that it's hard to change the way you do things when the method you're using is working. But the techniques I'm about to describe provide great flexibility and may allow you to streamline some processes.

Generating a user profile report in the past always required use of the age-old technique of running DSPUSRPRF *ALL OUTFILE(yourlib/yourfile) to generate a file containing information about all profiles on the system and then running a query (*QRYDFN) against that file to get the desired results. This chapter is about replacing that method with running SQL over the USER_INFO view in the library QSYS2.

Why? Because the information is always up to date. Delete a profile, and the view is updated without any action on your part. Same for creating or changing a profile. How many times have you run a query and realized you were running it against old data? If for no other reason, you need to switch your process so you can be assured you're running against the most current information. Another reason to use QSYS2.USER_INFO is to make analysis easier by combining relevant information rather than having to manually combine the output from several IBM commands. Finally, modernizing your processes using IBM i Services often allows you to tap into resources that may not be familiar to users of IBM i. I worked with a Python programmer at one client who was very happy to write a script to access QSYS2.USER_INFO to gather user profile information from multiple partitions and consolidate it into one database. The consolidated database was then used by the company's compliance group to perform user profile analysis, which had previously been a very arduous and often error-filled task. I understand change is hard, but I encourage you to give these methods a try.

Analyzing User Profiles

It's always good to begin at the beginning, so let's do that.

Basic Information

Let's start with the basics: SQL that mimics DSPUSRPRF *ALL to an outfile. Launch Access Client Solutions (ACS) and then click on Run SQL Scripts. When the window opens, type this:

```
SELECT * from QSYS2.USER_INFO;
```

This Select statement provides information about all of the user profiles on the system. Scroll to the right to see which fields you can report on/analyze. Of course, you can download the whole thing into a spreadsheet (as I described in chapter 1) and analyze it from there, but I'm going to suggest some qualifications to the Select statement above to get to the information you're looking for more quickly.

You can also use the QSYS2.USER_INFO_BASIC service to get user profile information if you have a large number of profiles on your system and you're trying to optimize performance. It will return the same information as QSYS2.USER_INFO except that it will not include the USER_OWNER , USER_CREATOR, SIZE, CREATION_ TIMESTAMP, LAST_USED_TIMESTAMP, DAYS_USED_COUNT, and LAST_ RESET_TIMESTAMP fields.

I continue to see organizations analyze user profiles based on their user class. This method drives me crazy because the user class is not used when access to an object is checked. So thinking a user is in the "wrong" user class is really a waste of time unless you're moving the system off of QSECURITY level 20. For that example, see chapter 3. Instead, here are examples of some of the analyses I'd perform.

Special Authorities

The following example lists profiles having a specific special authority. In the example below, it's *ALLOBJ. (Simply replace *ALLOBJ with another special authority, such as *SECADM, to get that list.) The profile will be listed regardless of whether the special authority is assigned to the profile itself or is inheriting the special authority via one of its groups. I recommend this list be reviewed at least once a quarter to ensure profiles still require each special authority assigned. Similar to reviewing the members of each group, reviewing the list of profiles with each special authority will catch users who have changed roles as well as catch special authorities that may have inadvertently been assigned to a group and are now available to all group members.

The code below started out as one of the examples provided with ACS (as described in chapter 1), but I've modified it to select different fields that better fit the profile attributes I find helpful for this review.

```
SELECT user_name,
       special_authorities,
       group_profile_name,
       supplemental_group_list,
       text_description
    FROM QSYS2.USER_INFO
    WHERE SPECIAL_AUTHORITIES LIKE '%*ALLOBJ%'
        OR USER_NAME IN (SELECT USER_PROFILE_NAME
                FROM QSYS2.GROUP_PROFILE_ENTRIES
                WHERE GROUP_PROFILE_NAME IN (SELECT USER_NAME
                        FROM QSYS2.USER_INFO
                        WHERE SPECIAL_AUTHORITIES LIKE '%*ALLOBJ%'))
    ORDER BY USER_NAME;
```

Note

The first field that I've selected in this SQL is user_name. That's the system name of the field (sometimes known as the "short name" because it will be at most only 10 characters long). The SQL name for this field is authorization_name which, in my opinion, is not very descriptive. So I've mixed system name and SQL names for the names of the fields I'm selecting. I'm pointing this out because, prior to writing this book, I didn't realize you could use both types in the same SQL statement! I encourage you to make your SQL as readable (and thus, self-documenting) as possible.

Limited Capabilities

You may also want to look at attributes such as the limited capability setting. Your review would be to make sure that any profile set to limited *PARTIAL or *NO really has a job requirement to use a command line.

```
SELECT user_name,
       special_authorities,
       group_profile_name,
       supplemental_group_list,
       limit_capabilities,
       text_description
    FROM QSYS2.USER_INFO
    WHERE LIMIT_CAPABILITIES <> '*YES';
```

Inactive Profiles

Finally, inactive profiles need to be managed so they can't be used as a target of abuse. Some organizations use the Analyze Profile Activity function from the SECTOOLS menu to set profiles to the status of disabled after a period of time. But often, organizations want to manage the disabling and deletion of profiles themselves. Even if you have automated these processes, reviewing the list produced by the SQL below can assure that your processes are working. In addition, automated processes usually have some type of "omission" list so that profiles will never be touched by the automated process. It's good to review that omission list so you don't continue to omit profiles that really should now be set to the status of disabled or even removed from the system. The following SQL lists all profiles that were created over three months ago and haven't been used in that timeframe.

```
SELECT user_name,
       last_used_timestamp,
       previous_signon,
       creation_timestamp,
       status,
       text_description
    FROM QSYS2.USER_INFO
    WHERE (last_used_timestamp IS NULL
          OR last_used_timestamp < CURRENT TIMESTAMP - 3 MONTHS)
        AND (creation_timestamp < CURRENT TIMESTAMP - 3 MONTHS);
```

You can do all sorts of creative things with timestamps. For example, some organizations want to disable a profile if, after creation, the user doesn't change their password within the first week. So you could do something similar to the previous example using the password_change_date and use "days" as the timeframe rather than "months."

Disabling Inactive Profiles

The SYSTOOLS.CHANGE_USER_PROFILE() table function provides more than just a list of inactive profiles. Depending on the value of the Preview parameter, you can have the table function set the profiles identified to be status of *DISABLED. Think about wanting to automate the disabling of profiles when they hit the criteria so that they are then considered inactive.

Running the example below, all profiles that have either never been used or haven't been used in three months and were created more than three months ago will be set to status of *DISABLED.

```
SELECT *
    FROM QSYS2.USER_INFO,
        TABLE (SYSTOOLS.CHANGE_USER_PROFILE(P_USER_NAME => USER_NAME,
            P_STATUS => '*DISABLED', PREVIEW => 'YES'))
    WHERE (last_used_timestamp IS NULL
        OR last_used_timestamp < CURRENT TIMESTAMP - 3 MONTHS)
        AND (creation_timestamp < CURRENT TIMESTAMP - 3 MONTHS);
```

You can review the list of profiles prior to the change by setting the Preview parameter to YES in the table function. Not all user profile attributes are included in this function (some notable ones that are missing include the supplemental group and special authorities attributes), but enough are included to make this useful and, hopefully, over time, IBM will provide a fully functional equivalent of CHGUSRPRF. In addition, it's likely you'd want to add another piece to that Where clause—that is, a list of profiles to which the change would never apply.

Profiles with a Default Password

The Analyze Default Password (ANZDFTPWD) is great, especially if you're just getting acquainted with IBM i, but I prefer to get information formatted in a way that helps me more easily analyze risk associated with those profiles.

Let's look at ANZDFTPWD. In addition to the name of the profile with a password that's the same as the user profile name, the report provides the profile's status (enabled or disabled), indicates whether the password is expired, and shows the text description, which is somewhat useful information, but if I have profiles with default passwords, especially a long list of them, I want more information so I know where to focus my efforts in setting that password to something other than the default. I want the special authorities so I can address the most powerful profiles first, group and supplemental groups so I can know if it has been assigned to a powerful group, status so I can focus on those that are enabled, last-used timestamp so I can understand if it's currently in use, creation timestamp so I know when it was created (recently or years ago), the creator so I can educate that administrator on the need to create profiles with a strong password, and the text description so (hopefully) I can have some idea what this profile is used for.

```
SELECT user_name,
       password_expiration_interval,
       special_authorities,
       group_profile_name,
       supplemental_group_list,
       status,
       last_used_timestamp,
       creation_timestamp,
       user_creator,
       text_description
    FROM QSYS2.USER_INFO
    WHERE user_default_password = 'YES'
      ORDER BY STATUS;
```

Yes, I could have gotten all of this information by first starting with ANZDFTPWD and then running Display User Profile (DSPUSRPRF) on each individual profile, but why do that when I can get what I need by using one simple SQL statement?

Analyzing Group Profiles
Now let's take a look at group profiles.

Members of a Group Profile

Reviewing the list of profiles assigned to each group is important in order to catch a user who has changed jobs and perhaps been assigned a new group profile but was left with their original groups to facilitate cross-training. To make sure users have access only to the information required to perform their jobs, their group and supplemental group assignments need to be reviewed regularly; I recommend at least once a quarter. To review all members of all groups, simply run this:

```
SELECT * from QSYS2.GROUP_PROFILE_ENTRIES;
```

If you want to focus on the members of one specific group, such as QPGMR, add a Where clause:

```
SELECT *
    from QSYS2.GROUP_PROFILE_ENTRIES
    where GROUP_PROFILE_NAME = 'QPGMR';
```

Group Profile Configuration

Group profiles aren't meant to be used for sign-on; therefore, there are several parameters I examine to make sure that can't happen or that the profile doesn't show up unnecessarily on reports (such as reports with non-expiring passwords or profiles that are limited capabilities *NO). Yes, you can visually examine the attributes of each group profile to make sure they're configured correctly, but I think this is much more efficient:

```
SELECT *
    FROM qsys2.user_info
    WHERE group_id_number <> 0
          AND ((status = '*ENABLED')
              OR (no_password_indicator = 'NO')
              OR (password_expiration_interval <> 0)
              OR (initial_menu_name <> '*SIGNOFF')
              OR (initial_program_name <> '*NONE')
              OR (limit_capabilities <> '*YES'));
```

Group Profiles Without Members

Note that I've used group_id_number <> 0 to find the group profiles. When a profile is made a group (that is, it's listed as a user's group profile or one of its supplemental groups), it's assigned a group ID (GID). Even after all of the members are removed from a group, it retains its GID, so in my opinion that's a better indication of profiles the system considers a group. That said, you may want to find the profiles that have retained a GID but have no members because the GID may be preventing the profile from being deleted. You can find that set by running the following:

```
SELECT user_name,
       text_description
    FROM qsys2.user_info
    WHERE group_id_number <> 0
          AND group_member_indicator = 'NO';
```

Other Profiles and Services to Consider

Now let's talk about those profiles that are created to perform a task. They don't represent a specific user. Often, they are created to facilitate a connection from another server or to run a scheduled job. Organizations have a variety of names for this type of profile, but I'm going to call it a "service account."

Service Accounts

Analyzing service accounts (that is, those profiles that run scheduled jobs and connect via ODBC from other systems such as Windows servers) will be a bit more tricky if you haven't used a naming convention. You'll have to name each profile in the SQL and run the analysis one profile at a time. However, even if you have to name each service account, you'll want to make sure they're configured correctly. Depending on its purpose, it may or may not have a password, but the rest of the attributes should be the same as group profiles. Here's an example of what the check may look like (where APPOWNER, JOBSCHED1, and ODBC2000 are names of service accounts).

```
SELECT *
    FROM qsys2.user_info
    WHERE user_name in ('APPOWNER', 'JOBSCHED1', 'ODBC2000')
          AND ((status = '*ENABLED')
```

```
     OR (no_password_indicator = 'NO')
     OR (password_expiration_interval <> 0)
     OR (initial_menu_name <> '*SIGNOFF')
     OR (initial_program_name <> '*NONE')
     OR (limit_capabilities <> '*YES'));
```

Owned Objects

I ran into a situation where a client was trying to delete a profile but couldn't because it owned objects. My client thought this was odd because the profile had been configured to have its group own any object it created. Even though a profile is configured in this way, I've found they can own objects, especially IFS objects since the IFS ignores that OWNER parameter in the user profile.

When organizations run across profiles they can't delete, I typically advise them to run Work with Objects by Owner (WRKOBJOWN) because it lists both objects in libraries as well as directories (unlike DSPUSRPRF *OBJOWN); it also gives you the option to change the ownership of those objects. But perhaps you'd like to be proactive and find out if profiles are owning objects, when, in reality, they shouldn't. Rather than run WRKOBJOWN for each profile, you can run the following SQL to find the list of profiles that own objects.

```
SELECT *
    FROM qsys2.object_ownership
    WHERE user_name LIKE 'CON%'
        AND object_type <> '*MSGQ';
```

Note

In this case, the set of profiles that weren't supposed to own objects started with a specific naming convention—in this case CON, but you can specify a specific name or even members of a group profile.

To get the list of objects owned by members of a specific group (in this example, GROUP1), you'd use the following SQL:

```
SELECT *
    FROM qsys2.object_ownership
    WHERE user_name IN (SELECT user_profile_name
                    FROM qsys2.group_profile_entries
                    WHERE group_profile_name = 'GROUP1')
        AND object_type <> '*MSGQ';
```

Note that I've eliminated message queues. Profiles always own their own *MSGQ. The message queue is automatically deleted by the system when the profile is deleted, so I didn't want those objects included in the list. I wanted the list of objects that would prevent the profile from being deleted.

Remember, if the result of running this SQL is too big to effectively evaluate it, you can always send the results to a spreadsheet. (See chapter 1 if you need a refresher on sending the results from Run SQL Scripts to a spreadsheet.)

I'll go into a deeper discussion regarding owned objects and what to do with them in chapter 7.

User Profile Changes in IBM i 7.5

Tech Note

IBM i 7.5 made several changes to the Create and Change User Profile commands.

IBM made several changes in IBM i 7.5 to the Create and Change User Profile (CRT/CHGUSRPRF) commands. The most obvious is that the PASSWORD parameter now defaults to *NONE rather than *USRPRF. In other words, the profile will no longer, by default, be created with a password that's the same as the user profile name. See Figure 5.1. Also, you will no longer get an error message if you specify the Set password to expired parameter (PWDEXP) to *YES and leave the User password field as *NONE. (In prior releases, this is an error that would have prevented the profile from being created.) This change is especially helpful if you've changed the command default for the PWDEXP parameter from *NO to *YES.

```
                         Create User Profile (CRTUSRPRF)
 Type choices, press Enter.

 User profile . . . . . . . . .   newprofile    Name
 User password  . . . . . . . .   *NONE

 _____
 Set password to expired  . . . . *yes          *NO, *YES
```

*Figure 5.1: Create and Change User Profile now defaults the PASSWORD parameter to *NONE rather than *USRPRF.*

Another change to CRT/CHGUSRPRF is the addition of the Maximum sign-on attempts (MAXSIGN) parameter. See Figure 5.2. It defaults to the value of the QMAXSIGN system value but allows you to override this and specify a different value for the number of invalid sign-on attempts that you allow before some action is taken. Note that the action taken is still governed by the QMAXSGNACN system value.

```
                         Create User Profile (CRTUSRPRF)
 Type choices, press Enter.


                         Additional Parameters

 Special authority  . . . . . . .   *USRCLS        *USRCLS, *NONE, *ALLOBJ...
               + for more values    _____
 Special environment  . . . . . .   *SYSVAL        *SYSVAL, *NONE, *S36
 Display sign-on information  . .    *SYSVAL        *SYSVAL, *NO, *YES
 Password expiration interval . .    *SYSVAL        1-366, *SYSVAL, *NOMAX
 Block password change  . . . . .    *SYSVAL        1-99, *SYSVAL, *NONE
 Local password management  . . .    *YES           *YES, *NO
 Maximum sign-on attempts . . . .    *SYSVAL        1-25, *SYSVAL
 Limit device sessions  . . . . .    *SYSVAL        *SYSVAL, *YES, *NO, 0, 1...
```

Figure 5.2: You can now override the QMAXSIGN system value at the user profile level using the MAXSIGN parm.

You may now want to look for profiles where the MAXSIGN parm doesn't default to the system value setting.

```
SELECT user_name,
       text_description,
       maximum_sign_on_attempts
    FROM qsys2.user_info
    WHERE maximum_sign_on_attempts <> '*SYSVAL';
```

Please resist the temptation to change your profile to specify a large number for the maximum number of sign-on attempts to avoid disabling your own profile. As an administrator, you should want to protect your profile as much as possible. Giving someone a lot of attempts to come up with your password is irresponsible since you likely have all power on the system. If you use this parameter, it should be used only for profiles that have very little authority and are using devices that may present difficulty in typing in a password—something like an RF device. That, or override it to a *lower* value for powerful profiles (including yours).

Users and Groups in New Nav

I've focused on using Run SQL Scripts, so let's switch and explore how to use New Nav to manage user and group profiles.

Launch New Nav, choose the partition to manage (called a "node" in New Nav), and then go down to the icon that looks like a group of people, as shown in Figure 5.3.

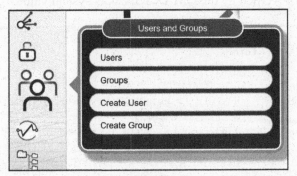

Figure 5.3: Move your cursor down to the "people" icon to access the Users and Groups section of New Nav.

The Create User and Create Group options are the same as they were in Heritage Nav. Create User is a graphical version of CRTUSRPRF together with the Add Directory Entry (ADDDIRE) command. Create Group is interesting, however, because it will create the user profile and then assign it as a group profile to the users you specify. In other words, in just one step, it creates the user profile and then makes it a group profile by assigning the members. If you want to create a new group in the green-screen interface, you have to run CRTUSRPRF to create the group (there's no separate command for creating a group profile) and then run CHGUSRPRF for each member and assign the newly created profile to each member's group list.

While creating a new group and assigning the members is much more efficient in New Nav, what I really want to draw your attention to are the Users and Groups categories. If you select the Users category, the result will be a listing of all profiles on the system (excluding group profiles). An initial set of profile attributes is displayed, but if you wish to see others, simply click on the three vertical dots (as shown in the upper right corner of Figure 5.4 below) to add or remove attributes to your view. Using the filters at the top of each column, you can investigate one specific profile or all profiles with *ALLOBJ or members of a specific group. For example, in Figure 5.4, all profiles beginning with CWOOD are listed. Under the covers, New Nav is using the QSYS2.USER_INFO IBM i Service to get the information. To see the SQL that's been generated, click on SQL in the upper right of the display. (Again, see Figure 5.4.)

Likewise, if you choose the Groups category, you'll see a list of the group profiles on the system. These two categories are very handy if you don't feel confident using SQL, want to see how the SQL is generated for a particular selection, or are already in New Nav and need to do some sort of user or group profile investigation and don't want to bother launching Run SQL Scripts.

Finally, you can highlight one or more profiles and click the Actions button. You have several actions to choose from, including listing the objects owned as well as exporting the information to a spreadsheet. Note that the attributes of each profile that will be exported are in the columns in your current view. So if you want all of the attributes of the profile, you'll need to add them to your view (using the three vertical dots) prior to exporting to a spreadsheet.

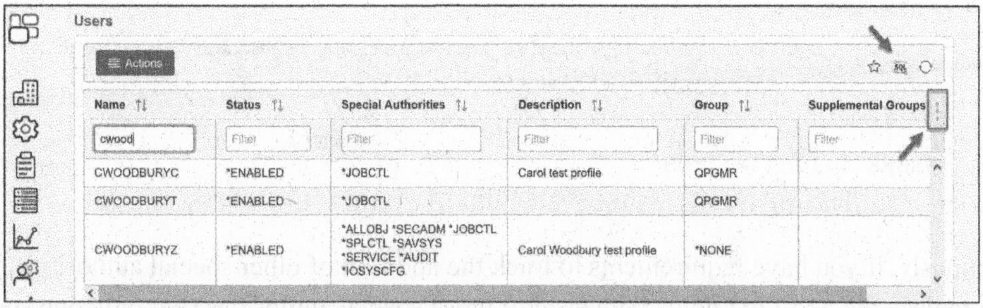

Figure 5.4: Filter the users by name or any other field. Click on the three vertical dots to add/remove attributes. Click on SQL to see the SQL generated by your selection.

User Profiles and the Audit Journal

It's one thing to analyze profiles at a point in time (which is what I've been describing so far), but many organizations need to understand user profile configurations over time. For example, some organizations have a requirement to track all profiles created so an auditor can look at a report and determine if the appropriate change request was in place to justify the profile being created. Or perhaps the requirement isn't for all profiles created. It may be for profiles created with a special authority, especially those created with or changed to have *ALLOBJ. I've also had clients who needed to track when profiles were deleted so there was proof that profiles were removed on a timely basis, especially when the individual was let go from the organization. Let's take a look at how the audit journal can help document your user profile processes.

Creation of Profiles with a Special Authority

The following SQL will provide you with a report of changes to profiles, so this will list profiles either created or changed to have *ALLOBJ when they didn't have that previously.

```
SELECT entry_timestamp,
       user_name,
       qualified_job_name,
       program_library,
       program_name user_profile,
       special_authorities,
       previous_special_authorities
    FROM TABLE (
            systools.audit_journal_cp(STARTING_TIMESTAMP => CURRENT
                TIMESTAMP - 7 DAYS)
        )
    WHERE allobj = 'YES'
          AND previous_allobj IS null;
```

Obviously, if you have requirements to track the addition of other special authorities, you can replace the ALLOBJ fields with each of those special authorities (but only one special authority at a time).

Another consideration is when a user is added to a powerful group. The following code looks at profiles where either the group or supplemental group fields were changed in the last 7 days and one or the other includes one (or more) of the powerful groups named (ADMINGRP, SUPERGRP, and QSECOFR). Obviously, you'll want to modify this to match your powerful group list. Note that you may get a false-positive result with this report because it's going to list the audit journal entry if there's *any* change to the supplemental group list. So if the supplemental group list contains one of your powerful profiles, it will be listed in the report, even if the change was to add or remove a different group. Unfortunately, IBM doesn't provide the previous group or supplemental group list in the audit journal entry, so I couldn't do a comparison like I could for the *ALLOBJ addition in the previous example.

```
SELECT entry_timestamp,
       user_name,
       qualified_job_name,
       program_library,
       program_name,
       user_profile,
       group_profile_name,
       supplemental_group_list
    FROM TABLE (
           systools.audit_journal_cp(STARTING_TIMESTAMP => CURRENT
              TIMESTAMP - 7 DAYS)
        )
    WHERE (group_profile_name IN ('ADMINGRP', 'SUPERGRP', 'QSECOFR'))
         OR supplemental_group_list LIKE '%ADMINGRP%'
         OR supplemental_group_list LIKE '%SUPERGRP%'
         OR supplemental_group_list LIKE '%QSECOFR%';
```

Finally, let's take a look at the profiles that have been deleted in the last month.

```
SELECT entry_timestamp,
       user_name,
       qualified_job_name,
       program_library,
       program_name,
       object_name,
```

```
      object_type
FROM TABLE (
          systools.audit_journal_do(STARTING_TIMESTAMP => CURRENT
              TIMESTAMP - 1 MONTH) )
WHERE object_type = '*USRPRF';
```

A reminder about the timestamp arithmetic: This example looks back one month, but if you don't have audit journal receivers on your system for the last month, the SQL can only bring back the entries for the receivers currently on your system. For example, if you only have audit journal receivers on your system for the last two weeks, this example will only report on activity for the past two weeks.

Enter a new IBM i Service that will help you with this! Shipping with IBM i 7.5 and available with IBM i 7.4 TR 6, QSYS2.JOURNAL_RECEIVER_INFO provides you with the journal receiver attach day and time so you can determine how far back your audit journal entries go.

```
SELECT TIMESTAMP(attach_timestamp, 0) AS curavlchn_start_time
    FROM qsys2.journal_receiver_info
    WHERE journal_library = 'QSYS'
          AND journal_name = 'QAUDJRN'
    ORDER BY attach_timestamp ASC
    LIMIT 1;
```

(Many thanks to Scott Forstie for this example.)

The takeaway: Make sure you set up your reporting schedule to match what you have on your system so you don't miss activity!

Examining the Audit Journal Using New Nav

New Nav provides a graphic way to view entries in the audit journal. Using the audit journal SQL table functions, audit journal entries can be viewed in New Nav. To access the entries, launch and sign in to New Nav, and then click on the padlock and choose Audit Journaling. You'll be taken to a window where you can choose the audit journal entry type(s) that you wish to see. See Figure 5.5. In my example, I'm going to uncheck the default entries selected and choose User Profile Changes (CP). Then I'll specify the date range of the audit journal entries I want to examine and click OK.

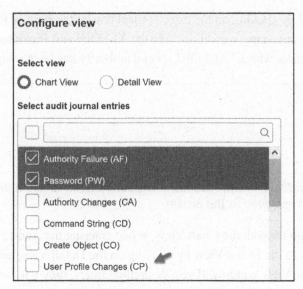

Figure 5.5: Choose the audit journal entry types you wish to see.

Because I left the view as the default of Chart View, the system now generates a chart of the number of CP entries over the time period I selected. See Figure 5.6.

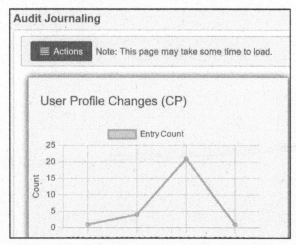

Figure 5.6: The Chart View shows the number of audit journal entries over the date range specified.

From here, I can right-click on the chart and choose Detail View to get the view as shown in Figure 5.7. Just like other categories in New Nav, you can customize which columns you want displayed by clicking on the three vertical dots at the right of the display. In this example, I've customized my view to include the ALLOBJ and Previous ALLOBJ columns so I can see the profiles where *ALLOBJ special authority has been assigned to the profile.

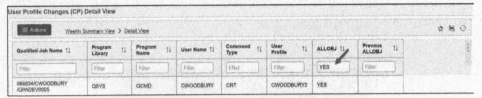

*Figure 5.7: User Profile (CP) audit journal entries are filtered to see entries where *ALLOBJ has been assigned to the profile.*

You don't have to go through the Chart View. When entering the Audit Journaling category, you can go directly to the Detail View by clicking on the Detail View radio button at the top of the Configure View window. If you've applied filters, they will be remembered and will be reapplied when you come back into the category. You can also "Favorite" this view by clicking on the star in the upper right of the display. Then access your Favorites by clicking on the building (Home) icon in the left navigation > Manage Favorites.

CHAPTER 6

Using Authority Collection to Reduce Users' Authority

IBM added the Authority Collection feature in IBM i 7.3. It allows you to start the collection on a specific user, specify the objects that you want to collect authority information for, and find out—from the operating system itself—what authority is required for the user to successfully access these objects. I've used this feature many times with clients, and it's incredibly helpful, especially when it's not obvious what all of the actions are that the profile is performing. The collection will tell me exactly which objects the profile is accessing, what authority is required, and the source of their current authority (e.g., group profile, *PUBLIC authority, adopted authority, authorization list, etc.).

I've found Authority Collection especially helpful when trying to reduce a user's authorities, particularly when the goal is to remove *ALLOBJ special authority. It's a fantastic tool at all security levels, but it's specifically useful when moving off of level 20 when you know that all profiles except those in the *SECOFR user class will have *ALLOBJ removed. More on that later in this chapter, but let's start with a simple scenario that applies at all security levels and to most clients I've worked with.

At all of my clients, there's been at least one service account that was created with *ALLOBJ because, at the time of creation, it wasn't clear exactly which objects would be accessed or (let's be realistic) the developer requesting the profile insisted it be created with *ALLOBJ! Now, with a greater emphasis on giving profiles only the authority they need and no more, my clients want to determine what authority this profile really needs. This is the perfect task for Authority Collection.

Authority Collection for Users: Objects in Libraries

First, you must start a collection for the profile you're going to investigate. Figure 6.1 shows the Start Authority Collection (STRAUTCOL) command. Specify the profile name and then the libraries containing the objects the profile accesses. The more you can scope down the objects for which you're going to collect information, the better, as there will be less to analyze. But if you truly have no idea what objects the profile touches, that's OK; specify *ALL for the library as well as leave *ALL as the default for both the Object and Object type fields. (I'll describe your options for IFS objects in a bit.)

```
                  Start Authority Collection (STRAUTCOL)

Type choices, press Enter.

Type of authority collection . .   *USRPRF        *USRPRF, *OBJAUTCOL
User profile . . . . . . . . . .   winsvr         Name
Library and ASP device:
  Library  . . . . . . . . . .    *all           Name, *NONE, *ALL
  ASP device . . . . . . . . .                   Name, *SYSBAS
               + for more values _
Object . . . . . . . . . . . .     *ALL           Name, generic*, *ALL
               + for more values
Object type  . . . . . . . . .     *ALL           *ALL, *CMD, *DTAARA...
               + for more values
```

Figure 6.1: STRAUTCOL collection being started for the WINSVR profile for all objects in all libraries.

Once you press Enter, the collection starts with the first action the profile takes. No need to stop/restart anything or to sign off/sign on. The collection just starts. Also, you're not going to see a job that's collecting the information if you run Work with Active Jobs (WRKACTJOB). That's because the collection is taking place below the MI (in SLIC) and is invisible to the operating system itself in much the same way that auditing is invisible.

Once you know that the profile has had some activity, start looking at the results. You may want to run the collection longer (perhaps over month end), but I recommend that you look at it sooner rather than later to start to get a feel for the type of information that's being collected and to start to understand how to read and interpret it.

Authority Collection information is viewed by running SQL against the QSYS2. AUTHORITY_COLLECTION view. I recommend that you start by looking at all of the entries that have been generated. Run the following, where XXXX equals the name of the service account you're investigating.

```
SELECT *
    FROM qsys2.authority_collection
    WHERE authorization_name = 'XXXX'
    ORDER BY system_object_name;
```

Scroll to the right. focusing on the column headings to see all of the information that's available and not so much on the actual results. Because you're analyzing a profile with *ALLOBJ, you'll notice that all entries list the authority source as *ALLOBJ, underscoring the fact that *ALLOBJ is the first thing checked in the authority-checking algorithm. See Figure 6.2 for an example. Once you remove *ALLOBJ, you'll see other sources, such as PUBLIC, GROUP PRIVATE, USER OWNERSHIP, etc.

```
157  -- Show authority source
158  SELECT authorization_name,
159         system_object_name,
160         system_object_schema,
161         system_object_type,
162         authority_source
163    FROM qsys2.authority_collection
164    WHERE authorization_name = 'WINSVR';
```

Authorization Name	System Object Name	System Object Schema	System Object Type	Authority Source
AUTHORIZATION_ NAME	SYSTEM_OBJECT _NAME	SYSTEM_OBJECT_ SCHEMA	SYSTEM_OBJECT_ TYPE	AUTHORITY_SOURCE
WINSVR	ALLOB00001	CAROLNEW	*FILE	USER *ALLOBJ
WINSVR	ALLOB00001	CAROLNEW	*FILE	USER *ALLOBJ
WINSVR	ALLOB00001	CAROLNEW	*FILE	USER *ALLOBJ
WINSVR	MAINT00001	CAROLNEW	*PGM	USER *ALLOBJ
WINSVR	QSQJRN	CAROLNEW	*JRN	USER *ALLOBJ

*Figure 6.2: Authority source will always be USER *ALLOBJ when analyzing a profile with *ALLOBJ special authority.*

Most of the information provided is invaluable, but I have to say that, in my opinion, IBM went a bit overboard and didn't need to include some of it because it only confuses the results. I'll explain as we go along. Let's start analyzing the results.

This may sound strange, but when I look at a profile's collection for the first time, I just kind of stare at it for a bit to try to get a big picture of what it's telling me. It will tell me what I'm interested in as well as what I can start filtering out.

One of the first sets of entries I filter out are the entries that indicate that the operating system's adopted authority will be used for the profile to gain access once the profile's *ALLOBJ is removed. You may not realize it, but much of the operating system adopts its owner (QSYS). That's so operating system tasks can be performed without the user profile requiring authority. Once a profile's *ALLOBJ is removed, the operating system's adopted authority will be used. So I want to remove those because you can be assured that access will be successful since the operating system will be taking care of the access. In fact, the following statement eliminates all program adoption because you also don't want to include programs you may have written that adopt authority or vendor products that adopt.

```
SELECT *
    FROM qsys2.authority_collection
    WHERE authorization_name = 'WINSVR'
        AND current_adopted_authority IS NULL;
```

The next set of entries to eliminate are the ones where the process is checking to see if the process has any authority to an object before proceeding to further access the object. I know the operating system does this, and I've also seen vendor products take this approach. The problem with the Authority Collection entries representing this check are the values shown in the Required Authority and Detailed Required Authority columns. Stating that the required authority is *ALL and listing all authorities, including *OWNER, in the detail field is incredibly misleading. See Figure 6.3. The system doesn't care what authority the user has; they are simply required to have one of the authorities. This is one of those entries that IBM (again, in my opinion) shouldn't have included in the collection. It's worthless information and, worse, is very confusing, so I'm going to eliminate that and reduce the confusion.

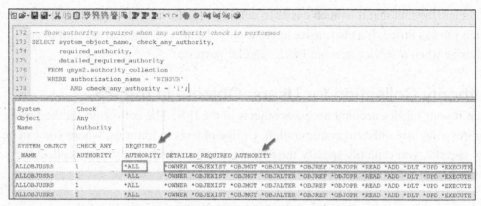

Figure 6.3: Checking for "ANY AUTHORITY" produces a highly misleading entry in the Authority Collection.

```
SELECT *
    FROM qsys2.authority_collection
    WHERE authorization_name = 'WINSVR'
    AND check_any_authority = '0'
    AND current_adopted_authority IS NULL;
```

Now you have a list of objects that the profile (in my case, WINSVR) is accessing where, once you remove its *ALLOBJ, access may be denied. Your next task is to determine where the profile's authority is going to come from once *ALLOBJ is removed. At this point, it may help to take a look at the job information provided with each entry. That information is toward the end of the entry, just before the path (IFS) fields. You may find, for example, that the profile is making an ODBC connection to access several database files. In this case, you could either grant the profile a private authority to those files or create an authorization list, secure the files with it, and grant the required authority to the list. Or you could make the access via an *SQLPKG, which could be configured to be owned by and adopt the profile that owns or is authorized to the database files.

If you have a service account whose purpose is not clear—that is, it's been overloaded and performs multiple tasks representing multiple roles—now may be the time to create more profiles and split up the tasks between new, single-purpose service accounts. When taking this approach with my clients, I've found that after the profile "break up," they all appreciate the fact that it's much easier to debug job failures as it's much more obvious which job has failed. It's also easier to grant only the access required and not over-authorize when a service account has a singular purpose.

Authority Collection for Users: Objects in the IFS

What if your service account accesses objects in the IFS? The collection for the profile requires a slightly different configuration. Unlike objects in libraries, where you can be very specific, you can only specify the object types for which you wish to collect the profile's access. See Figure 6.4.

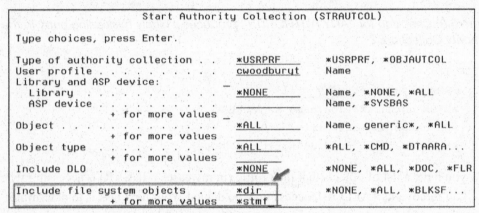

```
                    Start Authority Collection (STRAUTCOL)

 Type choices, press Enter.

 Type of authority collection . .    *USRPRF        *USRPRF, *OBJAUTCOL
 User profile . . . . . . . . . .    cwoodburyt     Name
 Library and ASP device:          _
   Library  . . . . . . . . . . .    *NONE          Name, *NONE, *ALL
   ASP device . . . . . . . . . .                   Name, *SYSBAS
                 + for more values _
 Object . . . . . . . . . . . . .    *ALL           Name, generic*, *ALL
                 + for more values
 Object type  . . . . . . . . . .    *ALL           *ALL, *CMD, *DTAARA...
                 + for more values
 Include DLO  . . . . . . . . . .    *NONE          *NONE, *ALL, *DOC, *FLR

 Include file system objects  . .    *dir           *NONE, *ALL, *BLKSF...
                 + for more values    *stmf
```

Figure 6.4: STRAUTCOL for user CWOODBURYT for all directory and stream file objects.

By the way, while I've separated out the analysis of which objects a user is accessing in a library versus IFS objects, I did so to make my examples easier. There's nothing technical stopping you from configuring to collect the access of both at the same time.

The approach for analyzing what's collected is the same as when the profile accesses objects in libraries, with one exception. You don't need to eliminate the Authority Collection entries having to do with adopted authority because adopted authority is ignored by the IFS. As you can see in Figure 6.5, because we could only specify the object types we wanted to collect the access of and not specific paths, we get a lot of what I call "extraneous" entries. While you can check the *PUBLIC authority to be sure, entries for objects in /QIBM* directories should be able to be ignored because they're typically representative of access that's provided via *PUBLIC authority.

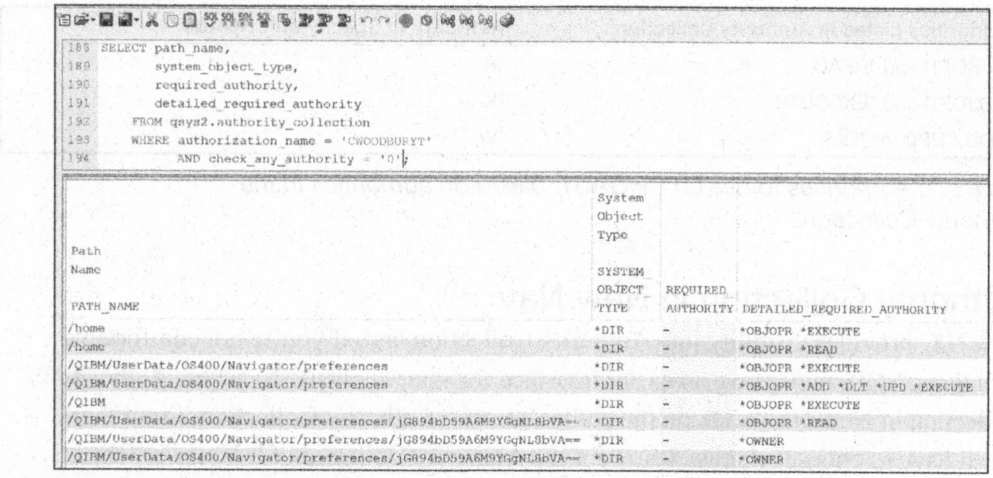

Figure 6.5: Authority Collection results when profile CWOODBURYT accesses *DIR and *STMF objects.

This SQL gets rid of access via the /QIBM directory and allows you to focus on the *DIR and *STMF objects to which the profile will need to have access granted if *PUBLIC authority won't be sufficient once *ALLOBJ is removed.

```
SELECT path_name,
       system_object_type,
       required_authority,
       detailed_required_authority
   FROM qsys2.authority_collection
   WHERE authorization_name = 'CWOODBURYT'
        AND check_any_authority = '0'
        AND path_name NOT LIKE '/QIBM%'
```

The other issue with the collection is that the authorities listed aren't the authorities you'll have to use on the Change Authority (CHGAUT) command. CHGAUT and any other command that sets authorities on IFS objects use *R (read), *W (write), and *X (execute) for the data authorities.

Here's a table that will help you make the translation from the authorities shown and what you'll have to set. (*OBJMGT, *OBJEXIST, *OBJALT, and *OBJREF are specified in the Object authorities for IFS objects and require no translation.)

Authorities Listed in Authority Collection	Authority to Specify on CHGAUT
*OJBOPR and *READ	*R
*OBJOPR and *EXECUTE	*X
*ADD, *UPD or *DLT	*W

Table 6.1: Authorities to use on CHGAUT, based on authorities in the Authority Collection.

Authority Collection in New Nav

New Nav provides visibility into Authority Collection and, if you're not comfortable with using SQL, may prove an easier interface for your analysis. To access Authority Collection in New Nav, click on the padlock icon > Authority Collection. From there, you'll have to choose whether you want the Authority Collection for Users or Objects. In this case, I chose Users. From there, specify the profile you're investigating and then choose the information you want to view. If you want all of that user's entries, choose View Collection. Just like all other New Nav windows, if you want different columns, click on the three vertical dots and adjust to your preference. That preference will be remembered going forward.

You may find handy what I call "shortcut filters." Rather than seeing all entries (by choosing View Collection), perhaps I want to see the directories the profile is accessing. In this example, I chose IFS directories. Figure 6.6 shows the summary of the directories accessed by the profile CWOODBURYT.

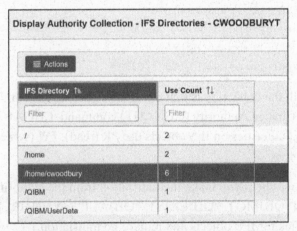

Figure 6.6: Choose IFS Directories from Authority Collection for a User to see the summary of directories accessed.

Notice the /QIBM/ entries that I mentioned in my earlier example. Using this view, I can ignore those and focus on the directories I want to secure. Highlight the directory, right-click, and choose Show All Items to see the entries for that specific directory.

Using Authority Collection to Prepare to Move Off of QSECURITY 20

If you're using this process to determine how to remove *ALLOBJ from regular application users running security level 20, I'm going to suggest that you first determine whether you're going to rework your application's entire security scheme (perhaps to use adopted authority to access database files) or you're going to only secure the files and directories containing the most critical information.

If you're going to rework your application's security design, I suggest that you do that first, prior to ever looking at the Authority Collection. That way, you can eliminate the application programs that adopt from your analysis (as I described previously) and determine if you've gotten everything configured correctly. Once you believe you have everything configured correctly, you can remove profiles' *ALLOBJ while the system is still at level 20 and test your application.

If you are only going to secure a few objects, the analysis is easiest if you use the Authority Collection at the object level, which was introduced in IBM i 7.4. I'll provide detailed examples of that in the next chapter. You can use Authority Collection at the User level if you're simply trying to determine what a typical user's access requirements are. The benefit of Authority Collection for Objects is that it will record all profiles that access the object along with the authority required. To get the list of all profiles accessing the object at IBM i 7.3 and earlier, you'll need to turn on *ALL object auditing for the objects and examine the ZR (object reads) and ZC (object updates) audit journal entries. Or you can configure Authority Collection for every profile on the system, which is clearly not the most practical approach!

Authority Failure Occurs

When reworking your security scheme, you may miss something or a process may only run periodically and the access wasn't in the collection when you first did your analysis.

I'd encourage you to turn back to the collection to resolve this authority failure if it's not obvious how much authority is required. Yes, you can look in the audit journal for the AF entry, but that's not going to tell you how much authority is required. While I encourage you to delete a profile's Authority Collection when you make changes (such as removing the profile's *ALLOBJ), you can still easily find the entry for the new object and avoid confusing yourself with looking at all of the entries in the profile's collection by running the following, which looks for Authority Collection entries where the authority check was unsuccessful.

```
SELECT *
    FROM qsys2.authority_collection
    WHERE authorization_name = 'WINSVR'
    AND authority_check_successful = '0';
```

If you did end and delete the profile's collection, I suggest that you start the collection for the profile and name the exact object on which you've seen the authority failure. Then repeat the process that caused the failure, and your analysis very easy.

Which Profiles Have a Collection or Are Actively Collecting?

Over time, you may lose track of which users have a collection or for which you're actively collecting access. This SQL lists the profiles that have a collection or are actively collecting:

```
SELECT authorization_name,
       authority_collection_repository_exists,
       authority_collection_active
    FROM qsys2.user_info
    WHERE authority_collection_repository_exists = 'YES'
        OR authority_collection_active = 'YES';
```

You can also get this list in New Nav. On the Authority Collection by User display, leave the User Profile field at the default of All (or use the dropdown to set it back) and choose Summary under the Display Authority Collection Options column.

Final Guidance

Authority Collection is the best security feature IBM has added to IBM i since auditing back in V2R3. It may be overwhelming at first, but it takes the guesswork out of reducing a user's authority. So stick with it and remember this: If the information you're looking at doesn't make sense, it's likely that you've included too much information (such as operating system adopted authority). If you're looking at all of the fields in the collection and it's overwhelming, try eliminating those that just don't make sense to you. Or perhaps you haven't included enough fields. Maybe you haven't included the source of the authority and it's a group that you didn't realize the user was a member of. So if you've severely limited which fields you're examining, try looking at all of them to see if the bigger picture makes more sense. The information you need is there, but you may have to take a couple of tries to look at it in just the right way.

CHAPTER **7**

Object Authorities

I end this discussion about the core of IBM i security with an explanation of the interfaces available to discover and manage object authorities. As you probably have heard me say before, each of the three areas of IBM i security must be in balance to successfully implement your system's security scheme; many organizations pay a lot of attention to system values and user profile settings but ignore object authorities. Let's take a look at how you can discover permissions using IBM i Services and IBM i Access Client Solutions (ACS).

Object Authorities: IBM i Services for Objects in Libraries

The QSYS2.OBJECT_PRIVILEGES IBM i table function allows you to list a specific object's permissions. For example:

```
SELECT *
    FROM TABLE (
            QSYS2.OBJECT_PRIVILEGES('LIB_NAME', 'OBJ_NAME', '*OBJTYPE')
        );
```

But what I find more interesting and useful is the IBM i Service version of OBJECT_ PRIVILEGES, where you can select objects based on specific criteria. It's useful because this allows you to find those objects in your production libraries that don't meet your security model. In the following example, the SQL will return any file in the PROD_LIB library that isn't secured with the PRODAUTL authorization list, has *PUBLIC set to *AUTL, and is owned by PROD_OWNER.

```
SELECT *
    FROM qsys2.object_privileges
```

```
WHERE system_object_schema = 'PROD_LIB'
    AND object_type = '*FILE'
    AND ((authorization_name = '*PUBLIC'
            AND object_authority <> '*AUTL')
        OR authorization_list <> 'PRODAUTL'
        OR OWNER <> 'PROD_OWNER');
```

In addition to the examples provided in chapter 5 for managing user profiles, you can find all *USRPRF objects that aren't set to *PUBLIC *EXCLUDE. By default, profiles are created as *PUBLIC *EXCLUDE. Profiles set to *USE or greater pose a threat because anyone can use that profile to submit a job and run as that profile and, in so doing, potentially elevate their authorities. (Note: I've omitted the three profiles that are purposely not set to *EXCLUDE by IBM.)

```
SELECT *
    FROM qsys2.object_privileges
    WHERE system_object_schema = 'QSYS'
        AND object_type = '*USRPRF'
        AND authorization_name = '*PUBLIC'
        AND object_authority <> '*EXCLUDE'
        AND object_name NOT IN ('QDBSHR', 'QDBSHRDO', 'QTMPLPD');
```

Object Authorities: IBM i Services for Objects in Directories

To discover permissions for IFS objects, you'll use the QSYS2.IFS_OBJECT_PRIVILEGES. In the following example, you'll get the object permissions for all objects starting at the /home directory, including all objects in /home as well as all subdirectories. (Thanks to Scott Forstie for helping me with this example.)

```
WITH ifs_auts AS (
    SELECT path_name
        FROM TABLE (
                qsys2.ifs_object_statistics(start_path_name =>
                    '/home')))
    SELECT iop.*
        FROM ifs_auts,
            TABLE (
                qsys2.ifs_object_privileges(path_name) ) iop;
```

But, as with OBJECT_PRIVILEGES, you can add a WHERE clause to find objects
that don't meet your security requirements. The following SQL lists all objects in the /
prod_directory (and all subdirectories) not owned by PROD_OWNER and all directories
whose *PUBLIC authority is not set to DTAAUT(*EXCLUDE).

```
WITH ifs_auts AS (
        SELECT path_name
            FROM TABLE (
                    qsys2.ifs_object_statistics(start_path_name =>
                        '/prod_directory') ) )
        SELECT iop.*
        FROM ifs_auts,
            TABLE (
                qsys2.ifs_object_privileges(path_name) ) iop
        WHERE owner <> 'PROD_OWNER'
            OR (OBJECT_TYPE = '*DIR'
                AND authorization_name = '*PUBLIC'
                AND data_authority <> '*EXCLUDE');
```

Managing Permissions Using IBM i Access Client Solutions (ACS)

If you wish to manage permissions using a graphical format, you're going to have to use
ACS as New Nav currently has no way to view or manage permissions. But not to worry;
the interface in ACS is quite usable. In fact, I quite like the ACS interface. To use ACS to
manage permissions, launch ACS and then click on Integrated File System. See Figure
7.1. You'll use this interface regardless of whether you want to manage an object in a
directory or a library—not obvious, I realize. (Or you can manage permissions for objects
in a library via the Schemas category in ACS.)

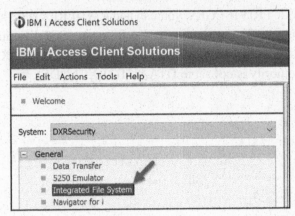

Figure 7.1: To manage permissions graphically, launch ACS and then click on Integrated File System.

This launches another window that will take you to the view of your /home directory. If you don't have a /home directory, it will take you to /root. To navigate somewhere other than your home directory, you can either type the path into the Directory field or use the up arrow to walk back up the path to the previous directory. If you want to manage an object in a library, no problem. Use the path /QSYS.LIB/your_library_name.LIB. See Figure 7.2.

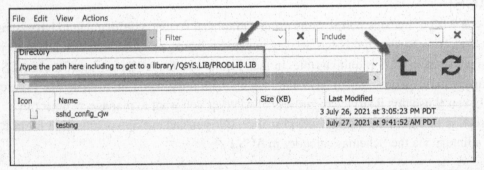

Figure 7.2: To get to the object you want to manage, either type the path in the Directory field or use the up arrow to walk back up the path.

Once you've navigated to the right object, right-click and choose Permissions. Another window will be launched, and from there you can modify all authorities. It's basically a graphical representation of Edit Object Authority (EDTOBJAUT). See Figure 7.3.

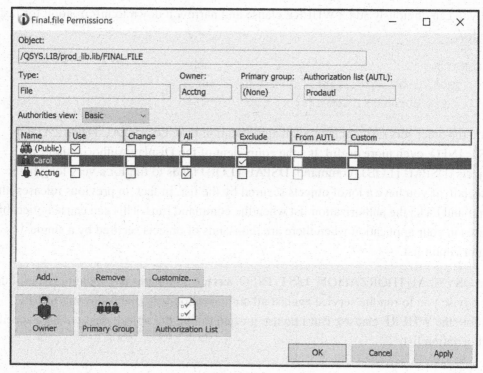

Figure 7.3: Permissions in ACS is the same as EDTOBJAUT.

Authorization Lists: IBM i Services

If you've heard me speak or read my articles, you know I'm a big fan of securing objects, especially database files, with an authorization list. Two IBM i Services are available for managing authorization lists.

QSYS2.AUTHORIZATION_LIST_USER_INFO is the equivalent of Display Authorization List (DSPAUTL) and shows all of the authorities associated with the list: owner, *PUBLIC, and the private authorities assigned.

If you run this SQL, you get the permissions for all authorization lists on the system.

```
SELECT *
    FROM qsys2.authorization_list_user_info;
```

But you can obviously add a WHERE clause and narrow it down to information for just one list.

```
SELECT *
    FROM qsys2.authorization_list_user_info;
    WHERE authorization_list = 'XXX';
```

I find the other service associated with authorization lists, QSYS2.AUTHORZATION_ LIST_INFO, even more useful. It's the equivalent of the Display Authorization List Objects (DSPAUTLOBJ) command. DSPAUTLOBJ tends to run for a very long time, especially if you have a lot of objects secured by the list. In fact, in previous releases, the command locks the authorization list when the command runs. This can cause noticeable pauses in your application when there are thousands of objects secured by a single authorization list.

The QSYS2.AUTHORZATION_LIST_INFO service eliminates any locking issues. I do *not* advise you to run the service against all authorization lists (the following SELECT without the WHERE clause). But I do use it often to find the objects secured by a specific authorization list.

```
SELECT *
    FROM qsys2.authorization_list_info
    WHERE authorization_list = 'XXX';
```

Authorization Lists: New Nav

To manage authorization lists in New Nav, click on the padlock icon and choose Authorization Lists as shown in Figure 7.4. You'll see that all permissions for all authorization lists are displayed. That's because what IBM has done is run the QSYS2. AUTHORIZATION_LIST_USER_INFO for all autls and displayed the results. To be honest, this isn't all that helpful. Yes, you can narrow down the results by specifying a particular authorization list, but I find this view and the output from QSYS2. AUTHORIZATION_LIST_USER_INFO to be no better than running DSPAUTL from a command line. But it's worse in one way because I can run Edit Authorization List (EDTAUTL) and change the permissions. One handy aspect of this view is that you can highlight one entry and either right-click or choose Actions and get the objects secured by the list. Again, all that's been done is to run the QSYS2.AUTHORZATION_LIST_INFO service for a specific autl. Hopefully, at some point in the future, IBM will add more functionality to this authorization list category, such as the ability to modify permissions.

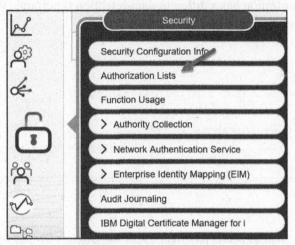

Figure 7.4: Manage authorization lists in New Nav by clicking on the padlock icon.

Object Statistics: Objects in Libraries

While it may not be obvious, the QSYS2.OBJECT_STATISTICS table function can help manage your security implementation. Building from the example I provided in chapter 5, where I discussed the inability to delete a profile due to its owning objects, we can use OBJECT_STATISTICS to perform more investigation. Rather than just reassigning those owned objects to another profile, I'd rather identify objects that haven't been used in a while and remove them from the system.

The OBJECT_STATISTICS table function is the equivalent of Display Object Description (DSPOBJD). But unlike DSPOBJD, I can customize the SQL to give me information on objects in libraries that are owned by a specific profile. The following example lists the objects owned by profile CAROL.

```
SELECT *
    FROM TABLE (
            QSYS2.OBJECT_STATISTICS('*ALL', '*ALL')
        )
    WHERE OBJOWNER = 'CAROL';
```

Then, I can add a WHERE clause that will allow me to see objects in libraries that have not been used within the last year and would, therefore, be a candidate for deletion. (Of course, if your organization has a different data-retention timeframe, you can alter the SQL timestamp math to match that.)

```
SELECT *
    FROM TABLE (
            QSYS2.OBJECT_STATISTICS('*ALL', '*ALL')
        )
    WHERE objowner = 'CAROL'
        AND (last_used_timestamp < CURRENT TIMESTAMP - 1 YEAR);
```

Note

If all you wish to see is a simple list of the objects owned by a user, a *much* better-performing option is to use QSYS2.OBJECT_OWNERSHIP.

Object Statistics: Objects in Directories

For IFS object information, you'll have to use the QSYS2.IFS_OBJECT_STATISTICS table function. The following example will list the objects owned by CAROL in the directory you specify. I should have warned you that the previous example may run awhile when you leave the first parameter (the library parameter) as *ALL. In the following example, if you specify the /root directory for the path name and you store many objects in the IFS as some organizations do, you'll have to be prepared for this to run *a long time!* Therefore, you may want to scope this selection down to a directory where you know the profile owns objects.

```
SELECT *
    FROM TABLE (
            QSYS2.IFS_OBJECT_STATISTICS(START_PATH_NAME =>
                '/dir-name', SUBTREE_DIRECTORIES => 'YES')
        )
    WHERE object_owner = 'CAROL';
```

And just like objects in libraries, timestamp arithmetic works for the IFS objects as well:

```
SELECT *
    FROM TABLE (
            QSYS2.IFS_OBJECT_STATISTICS(START_PATH_NAME =>
                '/dir-name', SUBTREE_DIRECTORIES => 'YES')
        )
    WHERE object_owner = 'CAROL'
            AND (last_used_timestamp < CURRENT TIMESTAMP - 6 months);
```

Object Statistics: Last_used_object Field

Note

Be careful when you're evaluating *DIR objects. The last-used date isn't updated. In other words, you must evaluate the objects *in* the directory to discover the correct last-used date. In fact, this is where the field last_used_object recently added to both QSYS2.OBJECT_STATISTICS and QSYS2.IFS_OBJECT_STATISTICS table functions is handy. It provides an indication of whether the object's last-used date is updated. A value of YES means that the last-used date is updated whenever the object is used. NO means it's not, so you shouldn't use the last-used date to determine whether you can delete the object based on usage.

Tech Note

As of IBM i 7.5, information about *USRPRF objects will not be returned by interfaces such as QSYS2.OBJECT_STATISTICS unless the profile running the service has some authority (not *EXCLUDE) to the profile.

Protect Information from Appearing in the Plan Cache and Database Monitors

While the tools IBM provides for database analysis are invaluable for tasks such as performance analysis, one problem is that they may contain data that people performing the analysis shouldn't be allowed to see. To protect sensitive information, you can use the sysproc.set_column_attribute procedure to set the column in a database file so that the contents won't appear in either a database monitor or plan cache. Be aware that running this takes action! It's not an "info only" service. Running the following will set the CCNBR column in the Orders file in the LIB1 library so that its contents will not be listed in the plan cache and database monitors. Rather, the variable values will be shown as *SECURE.

```
CALL SYSPROC.SET_COLUMN_ATTRIBUTE('LIB1', 'ORDERS', 'CCNBR',
    'SECURE YES');
```

You can use qsys2.syscolumns2 to see which columns have set this attribute.

Using the Audit Journal

Let's look at some of the ways the audit journal can help you.

Authority Failure (AF)

There's a variety of ways to use the audit journal in the context of object authorities, the most obvious being the Authority Failure (AF) entries. I used the AF entries in an earlier chapter to look for issues prior to moving to QSECURITY level 40. But in this context, you'd likely be using the AF entry to determine the actual object the process failed on. Many of you are probably saying, "I just look in the joblog for the object name. Why would I want or need to look in the audit journal?" Good question! Many times, the object name in the joblog is correct. But I've had cases where there had been an authority failure, but the process kept running and the authority failure appearing in the joblog was three to four steps after the actual failure. So attempting to solve the authority failure for the object stated in the joblog was futile. That's why, as a rule, when I'm debugging an authority failure, I'm going to look in the audit journal to verify that I'm debugging the right issue.

Options for Getting Entries out of the Audit Journal

Getting to the right audit journal entry in this case is usually very easy. You have the timeframe in the joblog, so you can narrow down which audit journal entries are collected. You may not even have to add a WHERE clause to your SQL to get to the right entry.

You have three options for getting to the information you need:

Option #1: Green-screen commands

```
CPYAUDJRNE ENTTYP(AF) JRNRCV(*CURCHAIN) - F4 - specify the date and
    time range shortly before and after the failure.
STRSQL
SELECT AFTSTP, AFJOB, AFUSER, AFNBR, AFPGM, AFPGMLIB, AFUSPF,
AFVIOL, AFONAM, AFOLIB, AFOTYP FROM qtemp/qauditaf
```

The object receiving the first authority failure in the failing process is in the AFONAM field and the library in the AFOLIB field. The program running at the time of the process is AFPGMLIB/AFPGM. With this information, you should be able to resolve the authority failure.

Option #2: The systools.audit_journal_af table function

AF is one of the audit types provided as an SQL table function, so alternatively (and preferably) from Run SQL Scripts you can run this:

```
SELECT entry_timestamp,
       user_name,
       qualified_job_name,
       program_library,
       program_name,
       violation_type,
       violation_type_detail,
       object_library,
       object_name,
       object_type
    FROM TABLE (systools.audit_journal_af(
    STARTING_TIMESTAMP => CURRENT TIMESTAMP - 14 DAYS ))
    WHERE violation_type IN ('A', 'K');
```

Option #3: New Nav

Click on the padlock icon and choose Audit Journaling. In the Configure view window, click on Detail View, and then select Authority Failure (AF) and specify the date/time range. Click OK. The entries created during that timeframe will be displayed. See Figure 7.5. The Object Name and Object Library columns will provide the object on which the failure occurred, and the Program Library and Program Name columns will tell you what program was running at the time the audit journal entry was generated.

Authority Failure (AF) Detail View							
☰ Actions Daily Summary View ❯ Detail View							
Qualified Job Name ↑↓	Program Library ↑↓	Program Name ↑↓	User Name ↑↓	Object Library ↑↓	Object Name ↑↓	Object Type ↑↓	
Filter	Filter	Filter	Filter	Filter	Filter	Filter	
078137/CWOODBURYT /QPADEV0005	QSYS	QCMD	CWOODBURYT	CWOODBURY	IADOPT	*PGM	

Figure 7.5: The Detail View of the AF entries should provide the details you need to debug the issue.

Insufficient Special Authority

In addition to this example, another situation where you might get an AF entry is due to a user not having sufficient special authority. In this case, the AFVIOL (or violation_type) will be K. See Figure 7.6.

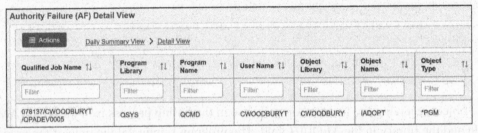

```
317   SELECT entry_timestamp,
318          user_name,
319          qualified_job_name,
320          program_library,
321          program_name,
322          violation_type,
323          violation_type_detail,
324          object_library,
325          object_name,
326          object_type
327     FROM TABLE (systools.audit_journal_af())
328     WHERE violation_type IN ('A', 'K');
```

USER_NAME	PROGRAM_ LIBRARY	PROGRAM NAME	VIOLATION _TYPE	VIOLATION_TYPE_DETAIL	OBJECT_NAME	OBJECT_TYPE
DEVELOPER	QSYS ...	QCMD ...	K	Special authority violation	CRTUSRPRF	*CMD

Figure 7.6: If the Violation_Type is K, it's an indication that the user doesn't have the correct special authority.

The action that the user was trying to take will be the OBJECT_NAME. In this case, the user tried to run CRTUSRPRF. Unfortunately, the audit entry doesn't list which special authority the user is lacking. The easiest way to determine that is to look in Appendix D of the *IBM i Security Reference* manual. Appendix D lists all CL commands provided by the operating system along with the authorities required to run them. When a special authority is required, there will be a footnote associated with the command that documents the special authority(s) required.

What if the authority failure occurred on an IFS object? No problem; we just need to look at different fields to get the path name. Path names are rarely 10 characters long, so rather than show a truncated name, the object name field will contain *N when you're looking at the audit journal via CPYAUDJRNE and STRSQL but will be NULL if you're using Run SQL Scripts. Here's the SQL for Run SQL Scripts:

```
SELECT entry_timestamp,
       user_name,
       qualified_job_name,
       program_library,
       program_name,
       object_name,
       object_type,
       path_name
FROM TABLE (systools.audit_journal_af(
STARTING_TIMESTAMP => CURRENT TIMESTAMP - 1 DAY ))
WHERE object_name IS null;
```

Other Audit Journal Types

Several other audit journal entry types can also help you debug issues or help you verify that processes are being followed when it comes to objects. These include OW (Ownership Changes), CA (Authority Changes), CO (Creation of Objects), and DO (Deletion of Objects). How you use these are limited only by your imagination, but here's an example of each to get you started.

Ownership Changes (OW)

Perhaps your earlier analysis via OBJECT_STATISTICS showed that one or more objects weren't owned correctly and you need to determine who changed the ownership and when. To determine that, use the OW audit journal entry. (To generate these entries, either *SECRUN or *SECURITY must be specified in the QAUDLVL system value.) Of course, the change would have had to happen within the timeframe of the audit journal receivers that you have on the system, but assuming that's the case, this will give you the information you need. The following lists the entries where the previous owner is PROD_ OWNER but was changed within the last week.

```
SELECT entry_timestamp,
       user_name,
       qualified_job_name,
       program_library,
       program_name,
       object_library,
       object_name,
       object_type,
       new_owner,
       previous_owner
   FROM TABLE (systools.audit_journal_ow(
   STARTING_TIMESTAMP => CURRENT TIMESTAMP - 7 DAYS ))
   WHERE previous_owner = 'PROD_OWNER';
```

Authority Changes (CA)

As with ownership changes, if authorities are changed, you'll want to know. I didn't discuss this for the OW entries, but you'll typically want to narrow down your search because the operating system generates OW and CA entries every time you create an object. In other words, there are *lots* of OW and CA entries and you won't want to wade through them all to get to the information you're looking for. (To generate CA audit entries, you'll have to include either *SECRUN or *SECURITY in the QAUDLVL system value.)

The following will list the changes to authority for objects in the PROD_LIB for all profiles except the profile running the change-management process. Most organizations that I've worked with want authorities configured such that developers can't change authority to production objects. All changes should come through an approved change-management process; therefore, you probably don't want to list the changes made by the change-management software. I strive to eliminate "known" or "approved" entries and focus on the exceptions so that it's easier to identify things that shouldn't have occurred, so I've eliminated the authority changes made by the profile running change management.

```
SELECT entry_timestamp,
       user_name,
       qualified_job_name,
       program_library,
       program_name,
       object_library,
       object_name,
       object_type
FROM TABLE (systools.audit_journal_ca(
STARTING_TIMESTAMP => CURRENT TIMESTAMP - 7 DAYS ))
WHERE object_library = 'PROD_LIB' and
      user_name <> 'CHG_MGMT';
```

Creation of Objects (CO)

Likewise, objects shouldn't be created into production libraries except via change management. I had a client that looked for programs being created on production by anyone other than their change-management profile, and whoever did it had to have an emergency change-management ticket or justify their action! But let's look at a different scenario. The IBM-provided library QGPL has been fondly called Q Garbage Pail Library because it ships with *PUBLIC set to *CHANGE and a lot of "stuff" gets created into it and rarely cleaned up. So this client decided to take control of QGPL. As part of that project, they started to monitor the *FILE, *PGM, and *DTAARA objects created into QGPL so they could determine who created them and how the objects were getting created. To get this information, they examined the CO (Creation of Object) audit journal entries. (To generate these entries, you'll need to have *CREATE specified in the QAUDLVL system value.) This gave them the programs running when the object was created as well as the creator. The entry also contains an Entry Type field. A value of N means it's a new object. R indicates the object replaced an existing version.

```
SELECT entry_timestamp,
       user_name,
       qualified_job_name,
       program_library,
       program_name,
       object_library,
       object_name,
       object_type,
       entry_type,
       entry_type
    FROM TABLE (systools.audit_journal_co(
    STARTING_TIMESTAMP => CURRENT TIMESTAMP - 1 DAY ))
    WHERE object_library = 'QGPL' and
          object_type in ('*PGM', '*FILE', 'DTAARA');
```

Deletion of Objects (DO)

When an object gets deleted (accidentally or intentionally), it's often difficult to determine how it happened. The DO audit journal entry is just the ticket to get the information you need. (To generate these entries, you'll need *DELETE in the QAUDLVL system value.) I'd *much* rather use the audit journal table functions, and although the systools.audit_journal_do table function does exist, I'm going to use a different technique to underscore how easy these table functions are to use compared to what I'm about to show you.

This example shows how you can run CL commands within Run SQL Scripts. You can run any command simply by specifying CL: at the beginning of the line. Pretty cool, huh? While that's cool, the field names that you have to use and the fact that this is a two-step process rather than one swift one underscores why you should use the audit journal entry table functions whenever they're available. Note that some fields aren't available when using CPYAUDJRNE (such as the combined job field and the fields that provide the detailed description of the entry type). Also, I had to modify my JDBC settings in Run SQL Scripts (specifically the Translation settings) to enable the pathname to get translated into a readable format. I hope you see that it's *much* easier to use the audit journal table functions rather than CPYAUDJRNE when the table function is available. (I'll get down off my soapbox now.)

This example shows how you can find who deleted a *STMF (specified in the WHERE clause using the DOPNM field). As such, I'm looking at the pathname field rather than the object and object library fields.

```
cl: CPYAUDJRNE ENTTYP(DO) JRNRCV(*CURCHAIN) FROMTIME(*FIRST)
TOTIME(*LAST);
SELECT DOTSTP,
       DOJOB,
       DOUSER,
       DONBR,
       DOPGM,
       DOPGMLIB,
       DOUSPF,
       DOPNM
    FROM qtemp.qauditdo
    WHERE DOONAM = '*N'
        AND DOPNM LIKE '/put your pathname here%';
```

More Information

I'll be discussing how you can automate checking and changing the authorities on objects in a later chapter. Please continue to the next chapter to see how to use IBM i Services to manage adopted authority. I'll discuss using Authority Collection for Objects to help you reduce the permissions assigned to objects after that. Finally, if you need best-practices recommendations for object authority settings, see chapter 6 in *IBM i Security and Compliance, Third Edition*, and for a step-by-step approach for reworking an entire application's security scheme, see chapter 17.

CHAPTER 8

Adopted Authority

Of course, adopted authority is something that needs attention. While it's a great tool for providing authority via an application, it does have the potential to be abused, so review is warranted. I recommend that administrators regularly review the programs that are owned by and adopt a profile with *ALLOBJ special authority. In addition, many organizations have developed applications that adopt authority to provide users access to their applications, so they need to make sure application programs are configured correctly to provide that access. This chapter discusses both scenarios and ends with a discussion on configuring dynamic SQL statements to adopt.

Discovering Programs That Adopt a Powerful Profile

The commands Print Adopting Objects (PRTADPOBJ) and Display Program Adopt (DSPPGMADP) provide lists of programs and service programs that adopt a specific profile. PRTADPOBJ only goes to print, so I find that command to be of limited use. DSPPGMADP provides more options for output, including an outfile, but why not get the information you need all at once rather than sending it to an outfile and then running a query over it? QSYS2.PROGRAM_INFO provides the mechanism to do just that.

For example, you may want to get a list of all objects that adopt QSECOFR.

```
SELECT program_library,
       program_name,
       object_type
    FROM qsys2.program_info
    WHERE program_owner = 'QSECOFR'
        AND user_profile = '*OWNER';
```

And while examining the objects that adopt QSECOFR is good, you'll likely want to examine the objects that adopt *any* profile with *ALLOBJ. Note that I don't select profiles whose group has been assigned *ALLOBJ, just profiles directly assigned *ALLOBJ. When the authority-checking algorithm checks for adopted authority, it only checks for sufficient authority of the program owner, not the program owner's group(s).

```
SELECT program_owner,
       program_library,
       program_name,
       object_type
    FROM qsys2.program_info
    WHERE user_profile = '*OWNER'
        AND program_owner IN (SELECT authorization_name
                FROM qsys2.user_info
                WHERE SPECIAL_AUTHORITIES LIKE '%*ALLOBJ%')
    ORDER BY program_owner;
```

It's quite possible to have vendor applications on your system that have programs that adopt QSECOFR. While you can ask your vendor to justify why they've configured their application that way, you really have no control over them. But what you do have control over are your own applications. So you may want to focus on programs that adopt authority that are being promoted into your own application libraries. I've had clients that require special review of programs that are owned by and adopt a profile with *ALLOBJ and without approval are not allowed to be promoted. To ensure this process is being followed, you can look for programs that have been created in the last week (for example) that adopt an *ALLOBJ profile and make sure there's a corresponding promotion request/approval. What you may want to do on a weekly basis then is to look for programs promoted to your production libraries.

```
SELECT program_library,
       program_name,
       program_owner,
       create_timestamp
    FROM QSYS2.PROGRAM_INFO
    WHERE create_timestamp > CURRENT DATE - 7 DAYS
        AND program_library = 'PROD_LIB'
```

```
AND user_profile = '*OWNER'
AND program_owner IN (SELECT authorization_name
        FROM qsys2.user_info
        WHERE SPECIAL_AUTHORITIES LIKE '%*ALLOBJ%');
```

Application Programs

Just because a program is configured to adopt authority doesn't mean that the program owner has to have *ALLOBJ special authority. In fact, I encourage those who are reworking their applications to provide authority via adopted authority to configure the application's owner profile with *no* special authorities and especially not *ALLOBJ. Having all application objects owned by the same profile and configuring the application programs to adopt should provide sufficient authority. Therefore, you'll want to regularly check to ensure all programs in the application library are owned correctly and configured to adopt.

```
SELECT program_library,
       program_name,
       object_type,
       program_owner,
       user_profile,
       use_adopted_authority
    FROM QSYS2.PROGRAM_INFO
    WHERE program_library = 'DXRTOOLS'
        AND (user_profile <> '*OWNER'
            OR program_owner <> 'APP_OWNER')
        AND program_name <> 'INITIAL';
```

As you may see in this previous example, there could be exceptions to this, such as the initial program that puts up the menu and command line. I encourage organizations to *not* have the initial program adopt to prevent adopted authority from flowing out to the menu's command line and to commands that should be run using the end user's authority, not adopted authority.

In that case, the programs should be configured with the User profile attribute set to *USER (so the program doesn't adopt) as well as the Use adopted authority parameter set to *NO (so the program doesn't inherit the adopted authority from a previously called program). You can verify those values with this:

```
SELECT program_library,
       program_name,
       object_type,
       program_owner,
       user_profile,
       use_adopted_authority
    FROM QSYS2.PROGRAM_INFO
    WHERE program_library = 'PROD_LIB'
          AND program_name = 'INITIAL';
```

Dynamic SQL

Finally, dynamic SQL is used quite frequently today, and it's often the case that the dynamic SQL statement within the program should adopt authority just as the program it's in adopts authority. The problem is that that doesn't happen by default. Even when the program's User profile attribute is set to *OWNER, the dynamic SQL doesn't adopt. To cause it to adopt, you must set the Dynamic user profile attribute to *OWNER when the program is compiled. To discover a program's Dynamic user profile attribute, run this for OPM programs:

```
SELECT program_library,
       program_name,
       object_type,
       program_owner,
       user_profile,
       sql_dynamic_user_profile
    FROM QSYS2.PROGRAM_INFO
    WHERE program_library = 'PROD_LIB'
          AND program_type = 'OPM';
```

And use this for modules bound into ILE and service programs:

```
SELECT program_library,
       program_name,
       object_type,
```

```
        bound_module_library,
        bound_module,
        sql_dynamic_user_profile
FROM QSYS2.BOUND_MODULE_INFO
WHERE program_library = 'QSYS2'
        AND sql_dynamic_user_profile IS NOT null;
```

The Dynamic user profile attribute defaults to *USER, meaning that the Dynamic SQL statement doesn't adopt. If you want the statement to adopt, it used to be that your only opportunity to change it from *USER to *OWNER was when you compiled the program. If you didn't set it on the compile, you were forced to recompile the program. For many reasons, organizations may not want or be able to recompile. Thanks to the team at IBM Rochester, you now have another option. The QSYS2.SWAP_DYNUSRPRF procedure takes the current Dynamic user profile setting of the program that you pass in and flips it to be the other setting.

For example, if you discovered that DYNSQL200 in PROD_LIB has the Dynamic user profile set to *USER and you need it to be *OWNER, you could run the following and the result would be that the Dynamic user profile attribute would be set to *OWNER.

```
CALL QSYS2.SWAP_DYNUSRPRF('PROD_LIB', 'DYNSQL200', '*PGM');
```

More information about this procedure can be found here:
https://www.ibm.com/docs/en/i/7.4?topic=services-swap-dynusrprf-procedure

SQL Naming Conventions and Adopted Authority

A nuisance that you may not be aware of (I wasn't until writing this book!) is the fact that the naming convention used in your static SQL (as opposed to Dynamic SQL) determines whether the program or procedure containing the static SQL adopts. This is true whether it's created using SQL or a CL command such as Create SQL RPG Program (CRTSQLRPG).

As shown in Figure 8.1, the User profile parameter defaults to *NAMING. A little-known fact is that if the static SQL uses SQL naming (objects are specified using the library. object naming convention), the User profile attribute of the program or procedure will be set to *OWNER, meaning that the program or procedure will adopt! If the static SQL uses the System (*SYS) naming convention, the User profile attribute will be set to *USER, meaning that the program or procedure will not adopt. When running the CRTSQLxxx commands, you can override the User profile parameter, but most people don't.

```
                    Create SQL RPG Program (CRTSQLRPG)

Type choices, press Enter.

Package  . . . . . . . . . . . .   *PGM          Name, *PGM
   Library  . . . . . . . . . . .   *PGMLIB       Name, *PGMLIB
SQL path . . . . . . . . . . . .   *NAMING       Name, *NAMING, *LIBL
              + for more values
SQL rules  . . . . . . . . . . .   *DB2          *DB2, *STD
IBM SQL flagging . . . . . . . .   *NOFLAG       *NOFLAG, *FLAG
ANS flagging . . . . . . . . . .   *NONE         *NONE, *ANS
Print file . . . . . . . . . . .   QSYSPRT       Name
   Library  . . . . . . . . . . .   *LIBL        Name, *LIBL, *CURLIB
User profile . . . . . . . . . .   *NAMING       *NAMING, *USER, *OWNER
Dynamic user profile . . . . . .   *USER         *USER, *OWNER
```

*Figure 8.1: Whether the program adopts authority depends on the naming convention used by the static SQL contained in the program when using the default of *NAMING for User profile.*

I hope this raises the awareness of the importance of having objects owned by the proper profiles. It should also underscore my recommendation that application-owning profiles and developers should not have *ALLOBJ special authority! I also hope that this drives home the importance of monitoring for new programs that adopt authority and that appropriate code-promotion procedures be in place and followed.

CHAPTER 9

Successfully Securing Objects by Using Authority Collection, IBM i Services, and Auditing

The purpose of this chapter is to help you understand the technologies available to you to successfully implement object security. Reducing the permissions to an object has been hyped by the security software vendors as being too difficult. That's simply not true! And the benefit of securing objects is that those permissions are enforced regardless of how and when the object is accessed—whether via a program, command line, web application, ODBC, FTP, SSH, etc. So once you've gotten the permissions set, you can rest easy that the work you've done will always be applied.

Another myth is that if you decide you want to implement object authorities, you must implement them on every object on the system. Again, not true. Some organizations let authorities default, except for the handful of objects they know contain data that they can't afford to lose or they know falls under regulatory compliance requirements. Or they simply know that critical data needs to be secured and they don't have time to do anything else. So lest you think the only proper way to implement object authorities is to implement them on every object on the system, we're going to start with two simple scenarios: reducing authorities on a directory and reducing the authorities on a database file. I'm separating these two because the technologies used to discover current access and subsequently reduce permissions are often slightly different.

The title of this chapter includes the word "successfully." I believe that one of the reasons people don't attempt to implement object security is because they've tried previously and things went totally sideways. Likely that was before IBM provided us with the technologies I'm going to discuss in this chapter. Used properly, there should now be very few, if any, surprises or failures when implementing object authority. Let's get started.

Reducing Access to a Directory

Most of my clients have one or more directories that contain confidential information. It may be image files of canceled checks or medical images that are kept permanently. Or a directory that contains a running year's worth of receipts with Personally Identifiable Information (PII) or invoices or a directory that holds what I call a "transitory" file. It's usually a stream file (*STMF) that's regularly created by a scheduled job. The file typically contains payroll or tax or bank information that's then sent off the system via some method of secure file transfer. Do any of these examples sound familiar?

To successfully reduce access to a directory, we must answer two questions: Who's accessing the directory? How much authority do they need?

For those of you running IBM i 7.4 and later, this exercise couldn't be easier. For this scenario, we're going to use Authority Collection. Earlier I discussed how you can use Authority Collection to reduce a specific user's authority to an object by configuring Authority Collection for that user and determining how much authority they require to the objects they touched. In IBM i 7.4, IBM gave us another option and that's to configure Authority Collection on a specific object. This option allows us to determine all of the users accessing the object as well as the authority required.

Configuring Authority Collection on an object is a two-step process. First, you must configure Authority Collection on your object. Figure 9.1 shows how to configure Authority Collection for the '/home/carol' directory. I've just configured the collection for the directory itself, but you can start it for the objects in the directory as well as subdirectories if you specify *ALL for the Directory subtree parameter.

```
                Change Authority Collection (CHGAUTCOL)

Type choices, press Enter.

Object . . . . . . . . . . . . . >  '/home/carol'

Authority collection value . . . >  *OBJINF      *NONE, *OBJINF
Include dependent objects . . .     *NO          *NO, *LF
Directory subtree . . . . . . .     *NONE        *NONE, *ALL
Symbolic link . . . . . . . . .     *NO          *NO, *YES
Delete collection . . . . . . .     *NO          *NO, *YES
```

Figure 9.1: Configure Authority Collection for objects using the CHGAUTCOL command.

Next, if the Collection isn't already started for objects, you must run the Start Authority Collection (STRAUTCOL) command. IBM i 7.4 added a new parameter to this command to specify whether you're working with user profiles or objects. In this case, we're (obviously) working with objects. See Figure 9.2.

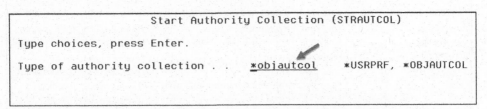

```
                Start Authority Collection (STRAUTCOL)

Type choices, press Enter.

Type of authority collection . .   *objautcol    *USRPRF, *OBJAUTCOL
```

Figure 9.2: Start the Authority Collection if you haven't done so previously.

Now you wait and let the Collection collect. How long do you wait before you look at the results? Again, as with user profiles, it depends. If you're securing a directory that you believe is only being written to by a scheduled job, let the job run and then look. But if you don't know, I'd let the collection run at least over a month-end before you can conclude your investigation is complete. (Obviously, you can look at the collection prior to month-end; just don't end it prior to that.)

To view the results of the Collection, you'll use QSYS2.AUTHORITY_COLLECTION_ FSOBJ (You need to use the view that corresponds to the type of object you've been collecting information on.)

Figure 9.3 shows the results. Notice that it only shows information for the directory you started the collection on, not the higher-level directories such as '/' or '/YYY' as the collection did when you were analyzing a profile's authority requirements via Authority Collection for profiles. The collection is very literal. If you said to start on the path '/directory/subdirectory', it will only collect for that specific path.

```
87  SELECT DISTINCT authorization_name,
88                  detailed_required_authority,
89                  path_name,
90                  job_name
91     FROM qsys2.authority_collection_fsobj
92     WHERE path_name = '/home/carol';
93
```

Authorization Name		Path Name	Job Name
AUTHORIZATION_NAME	DETAILED_REQUIRED_AUTHORITY	PATH_NAME	JOB_NAME
DEVELOPER	*OBJOPR *EXECUTE	/home/carol	QPADEV0003
DEVELOPER	*OBJOPR *ADD *DLT *UPD *EXECUTE	/home/carol	QZDASOINIT
DEVELOPER	*OBJOPR *READ	/home/carol	QPADEV0003
JOE	*OBJOPR *EXECUTE	/home/carol	QPWFSERVSO
JOE	*OBJOPR *ADD *DLT *UPD *EXECUTE	/home/carol	QZRCSRVS
JOE	*OBJOPR *READ	/home/carol	QPWFSERVSO
CAROL	*OBJOPR *EXECUTE	/home/carol	QZDASOINIT

Figure 9.3: Distinct accesses of the '/home/carol' directory.

Securing the Directory

Now that you have the results—in other words, the list of profiles accessing the directory—how do you set the authorities on the directory? Obviously, the profiles currently have access, but the goal is to secure the directory (as in set the directory to be *PUBLIC *EXCLUDE). Unless the profile has *ALLOBJ special authority and you intend to leave it with *ALLOBJ, you're going to have to ensure these profiles have sufficient authority. Here are some options:

- If you find the directory is accessed by only one profile, change the ownership of the directory to that profile and *PUBLIC to DTAAUT(*EXCLUDE) OBJAUT(*NONE), and you're done. Seriously. It's that easy. This is often the case with that "transitory file" scenario.

- If it's a situation where the directory contains six months (or choose your timeframe) of data and several people read that data, have the directory be owned by the process writing the information into the directory. This will help eliminate excess private authorities when the owner of the directory and objects in the directory don't match. Then, create an authorization list for the directory, put the users accessing the objects in a group, and authorize the group with only the authority required, which is likely to be *USE. Assuming the application was written to inherit authorities from the directory, as objects are created they will be secured with the authorization list to which the group is authorized, again reducing private authorities using an authorization list. If you grant a private authority to each individual requiring access, each of the profiles will have a private authority to each of the objects created into that directory—in other words, *lots* of private authorities, which you want to avoid so that your Save Security Data (SAVSECDTA) time doesn't get out of control. Also, this approach is terribly difficult to maintain, especially when you need to add a new user. If you use the "group profile authorized to an authorization list" approach, all you have to do when someone new needs access is to place them into the group. Once you've changed the ownership and secured the directory with the authorization list, don't forget to set *PUBLIC to DTAAUT(*EXCLUDE) OBJAUT(*NONE).

- If you find that several users are creating, deleting, and reading the information (in other words, the results are showing that they need the equivalent of *ALL authority), put those users in a group profile and change the ownership of the directory to the group. Then set *PUBLIC to DTAAUT(*EXCLUDE) OBJAUT(*NONE).

I rarely take the proactive approach to secure the objects in the directory. It's usually sufficient to secure the directory and leave its contents as is.

Reducing Access to a Database File

We'll use the same methodology for discovering who needs access to a database file as we did when securing a directory. First, identify the file(s) you want to secure. Then configure Authority Collection to start collecting information on who's accessing the file. Finally, start the collection (STRAUTCOL *OBJAUTCOL) if it hasn't already been started.

IBM did not provide separate commands for enabling Authority Collection on an IFS object versus an object in a library. You must specify all objects using a pathname. This is not difficult once you understand the convention. It's /QSYS.lib/your-library-name.lib/object-name.object type. See Figure 9.4 for an example.

```
                    Change Authority Collection (CHGAUTCOL)

Type choices, press Enter.

Object . . . . . . . . . . . . .   /qsys.lib/hr_info.lib/salary.file

Authority collection value . . . .   *objinf        *NONE, *OBJINF
Include dependent objects  . . .     *NO            *NO, *LF
Directory subtree  . . . . . . . .   *NONE          *NONE, *ALL
Symbolic link  . . . . . . . . .     *NO            *NO, *YES
Delete collection  . . . . . . . .   *NO            *NO, *YES
```

Figure 9.4: Configure Authority Collection for a database file.

For objects in a library, you can use either the QSYS2.AUTHORITY_COLLECTION_ LIBRARIES or QSYS2AUTHORITY_COLLECTION_OBJECT IBM i Service. One performs better than the other, depending on how many entries have been collected for the whole system as well as the specific entries you're looking for. Personally, I don't consider this a performance-critical function, so to me you can choose either one, and it really doesn't matter; the results will be the same. I've used the LIBRARIES Service to get the results in Figure 9.5. For an explanation of why I've removed the "adopted authority" and "check any authority" fields, see chapter 6.

```
 96  SELECT DISTINCT authorization_name,
 97                  system_object_name,
 98                  system_object_schema,
 99                  required_authority,
100                  detailed_required_authority,
101                  job_name
102     FROM qsys2.authority_collection_libraries
103     WHERE system_object_name = 'SALARY'
104           AND system_object_schema = 'HR_INFO'
105           AND check_any_authority = '0'
106           AND current_adopted_authority IS NULL
107     ORDER BY authorization_name;
```

Authorization Name	System Object Name	System Object Schema		Job Name
AUTHORIZATION_NAME	SYSTEM_OBJECT_NAME	SYSTEM_OBJECT_SCHEMA	DETAILED_REQUIRED_AUTHORITY	JOB_NAME
DEVELOPER	SALARY	HR_INFO	*OBJOPR	QPADEV0003
DEVELOPER	SALARY	HR_INFO	*READ	QPADEV0003
DEVELOPER	SALARY	HR_INFO	*OBJOPR *READ *UPD	QPADEV0003
DEVELOPER	SALARY	HR_INFO	*OBJOPR *READ	QPADEV0003
JOE	SALARY	HR_INFO	*READ	QZDASOINIT
JOE	SALARY	HR_INFO	*OBJOPR	QZDASOINIT

Figure 9.5: Distinct list of access of the HR_INFO/SALARY file.

Now that you have the list of profiles accessing the file you want to secure, you need to determine how you're going to secure it.

Application Access

If the file being secured is associated with an application, you'll see many, many more entries—those of end users accessing the file via the application. To secure the file, I'd suggest you identify which application programs are accessing the file and change them to adopt authority. In other words, set the User profile attribute of the program to be *OWNER. If the owner of the program is the same as the owner of the file and the program adopts, any caller of the program will have *ALL authority to the file. The easiest way to determine whether any application programs accessed the file would be to turn back to the Authority Collection. The following gets a list of the programs accessing HR_INFO/SALARY that are in the PROD_LIB library.

```
SELECT DISTINCT authorization_name,
                system_object_name,
                system_object_schema,
                most_recent_program_invoked,
                most_recent_program_schema
    FROM qsys2.authority_collection_libraries
    WHERE system_object_name = 'SALARY'
          AND most_recent_program_schema = 'PROD_LIB'
          AND system_object_schema = 'HR_INFO'
          AND check_any_authority = '0'
          AND current_adopted_authority IS NULL
    ORDER BY authorization_name;
```

This is the list of programs you'll want to consider setting to user profile *OWNER.

Other Access

For access to the file other than through the application, I suggest you attach an authorization list and authorize the profiles accessing the file via non-application interfaces to that list, granting only as much authority as identified in the Authority Collection. While you'll have to take an outage to attach the list, once attached, you can grant (and revoke) authority to the list at any time. Otherwise, you'll have to wait until the file isn't locked to modify the authority to the file. (A database file is locked when it's opened.) When attaching the list, I'd also set the *PUBLIC authority of the file to *AUTL, meaning that the *PUBLIC authority of the file is to come from the authorization list. That way, when you're ready to set the *PUBLIC authority to *EXCLUDE, you can do it and not wait for the file to be unlocked. More importantly, if things go terribly wrong for some reason after setting it to *EXCLUDE, you can quickly set it back to the previous value and, again, not have to wait until the file isn't in use.

Reworking the Authority Scheme of an Entire Application

I cover this topic extensively in chapter 17 of *IBM i Security Administration and Compliance, Third Edition,* but I wanted to mention a few things here. That chapter was originally written prior to Authority Collection being available. Some might wonder if I'd replace that guidance with the use of Authority Collection. The answer is no. To configure Authority Collection on all application objects, even if you limit it to just database files, I believe would be *very* overwhelming.

However, there is a place in this process for Authority Collection. Specifically, when reworking an entire application, the most likely to fail are processes that access data from outside of application interfaces, such as ODBC access from a Windows server or a secure file transfer to an outside source or a data transfer to a user's workstation. Once you discover these processes, you have to determine what authority to grant the profile to the database file in use, and that's not always obvious. If my client was running IBM i 7.4, I'd turn on Authority Collection on the objects identified as being accessed via non-application interfaces (ODBC, DDM, etc.) to determine how much authority is required and to make sure no other profiles need access. If they were running IBM i 7.3, I'd still use Authority Collection and turn it on for the profiles you've identified as accessing data outside of application interfaces. (The only difference between these two approaches is that you're not going to get the full list of profiles accessing the object when you turn on Authority Collection for the profiles versus turning it on for the object itself.)

How do I identify which profiles are accessing application data with some interface other than the application itself? As I describe in *IBM i Security Administration and Compliance, Third Edition*, it's a matter of turning on object auditing on the database files and examining the ZR and ZC audit journal entries to find the entries that are using a program other than an application program to read and/or update a database file. The other method you can use (if for some reason you can't turn on object auditing) is to examine the GR and GS audit journal entries. I don't describe examining those in the other book, so I'll describe them here.

This method is far less precise than using object auditing, but it will help you identify profiles using "external" interfaces (connections made from another system), perhaps a Windows server, a user's workstation, or even another system running IBM i. Then you can use Authority Collection for those profiles to discover the details of what they're accessing. One warning, however: You should not rely on this method as your sole means of investigation if you have two or more applications on your system that are "intertwined," meaning their use of data overlaps and they often pass data between them and/or share files and data. If you have this situation, you typically know who you are. This method will not catch a program from Application A accessing a database file in Application B's libraries, for example, and missing that information could mean that Application A could fail when it tries to access Application B's data if you haven't made accommodation for that access.

This method uses the GR (Generic Record) audit journal entries. These entries are generated if you've changed the default setting for anything in Application Administration (Function Usage). Little did IBM realize that, when they added the ability to control who can use ODBC using settings in App Admin, they were also providing an easy way to find out who's using ODBC! Same with FTP and DDM/DRDA.

GR audit journal entries are generated when you have either *SECCFG or *SECURITY specified in the QAUDLVL system value and have modified any Function Usage entry. Even if you simply change the default setting for who can access New Nav, for example, the system generates a GR record to log that the setting of the function was checked. While I couldn't care less whether it was checked or not, what this provides is a simple way to determine who's accessing the system via ODBC (function name QIBM_DB_ZDA), FTP (function names QIBM_QTMF%), and DDM/DRDA (function name QIBM_DB_DDMDRDA). The following gets all of these entries. I've included the IP address of the request in case you need to determine where the access originated.

```
SELECT entry_timestamp,
       user_name,
       program_name,
       remote_address,
       function_name
    FROM TABLE (
            systools.audit_journal_gr()
        )
    WHERE function_name IN ('QIBM_DB_ZDA', 'QIBM_DB_DDMDRDA')
        OR function_name LIKE 'QIBM_QTMF%';
```

Get the distinct set of access by profile.

```
SELECT distinct
       user_name,
       function_name
    FROM TABLE (
            systools.audit_journal_gr()
        )
    WHERE function_name IN ('QIBM_DB_ZDA', 'QIBM_DB_DDMDRDA')
        OR function_name LIKE 'QIBM_QTMF%';
```

To discover the use of SSH and QShell, use the GS audit journal entries and look for the job name of 'SSHD' and 'QSHSH' for QShell. (I describe in chapter 12 how to use the GS audit journal entries to discover who's using SSH.)

Once you find the profiles accessing the system using these various interfaces, you can turn on Authority Collection (as described in chapter 6) to determine which objects they're accessing. If it's files in the application you're securing, you know to add them to the list of profiles for which you'll need to grant authority.

Again, if you're reworking an entire application, I encourage you to read chapter 17 of *IBM i Security and Compliance, Third Edition* for more hints to help make your project a success.

Determining Where Authority Is Coming From

The final scenario is a situation where you thought you secured an object, but users are able to access it anyway. You've looked but can't determine where the users are getting their authority. As you can see in Figure 9.6, it appears that the HR_INFO/SALARY file should be secure!

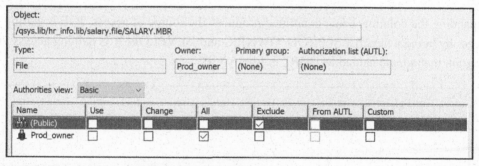

Figure 9.6: Permissions on HR_INFO/SALARY file.

Because the Authority Collection includes the source of a user's current authority, this is the perfect utility to help you debug this issue.

If the system is at IBM i 7.4, you can start the Authority Collection on the HR_INFO/ SALARY file itself. If at IBM i 7.3, you can start the Authority Collection on the users that are gaining access but shouldn't be. In this case, I configured Authority Collection on the file and then displayed the results. Figure 9.7 is a perfect example of my admonition that I gave at the end of chapter 6, where I said that if the results don't make sense, you need to look at less information or more. This is a case of needing more information. For example, how can DEVELOPER have access to the SALARY file if the current authority source is *PUBLIC yet *PUBLIC is *EXCLUDE?

```
152  -- Determine the source of access - file should be secured!
153  SELECT DISTINCT authorization_name,
154                  system_object_name,
155                  system_object_schema,
156                  current_authority,
157                  authority_source
158      FROM qsys2.authority_collection_libraries
159      WHERE system_object_name = 'SALARY'
160          AND system_object_schema = 'HR_INFO'
161          AND check_any_authority = '0'
162      ORDER BY authorization_name;
```

Authorization Name	System Object Name	System Object Schema		Authority Source
AUTHORIZATION_NAME	SYSTEM_OBJECT_ NAME	SYSTEM_OBJECT _SCHEMA	CURRENT_AUTHORITY	AUTHORITY_SOURCE
DEVELOPER	SALARY	HR_INFO	*EXCLUDE	PUBLIC
JOE	SALARY	HR_INFO	*ALL	GROUP OWNERSHIP

Figure 9.7: Showing the source of the access of HR_INFO/SALARY file.

Expanding the columns being examined produces the source of access. JOE is getting access by being a member of PROD_OWNER, and DEVELOPER is gaining access via a program that adopts named IADOPT in library CJW.

```
164  -- In this case, you must expand the results to determine where access is coming from
165  SELECT DISTINCT authorization_name,
166                  current_authority,
167                  authority_source,
168                  group_name,
169                  adopt_authority_used,
170                  adopting_program_name,
171                  adopting_program_schema
172      FROM qsys2.authority_collection_libraries
173      WHERE system_object_name = 'SALARY'
174          AND system_object_schema = 'HR_INFO'
175          AND check_any_authority = '0'
176      ORDER BY authorization_name;
177
```

Authorization Name		Authority Source	Group Name	Adopt Authority Used	Adopting Program Name	Adopting Program Schema
AUTHORIZATION_ NAME	CURRENT_AUTHORITY	AUTHORITY_SOURCE	GROUP_NAME	ADOPT_AUTHORITY _USED	ADOPTING_PROGRAM _NAME	ADOPTING_PROGRAM _SCHEMA
DEVELOPER	*EXCLUDE	PUBLIC	-	1	IADOPT	CJW
JOE	*ALL	GROUP OWNERSHIP	PROD_OWNER	0	QQQVFMT	QSYS

Figure 9.8: The expanded results show the source of access.

You can then expand the columns further to determine which profile owns the adopting program and that owner's authority and take the necessary steps to lock down that program. As far as JOE goes, this is an example of the risks you take when application users are a member of the profile that owns the application; they have *ALL authority to all application objects!

Which Objects Have Authority Collection Configured?

To determine which objects have Authority Collection configured, run the following for objects in libraries:

```
SELECT *
    FROM TABLE (
            QSYS2.OBJECT_STATISTICS('*ALL', '*ALL')
        ) AS X
    WHERE authority_collection_value = '*OBJINF';
```

And run this to determine the IFS objects.

```
SELECT path_name,
        authority_collection_value
    FROM TABLE (
            qsys2.ifs_object_statistics(start_path_name => '/')
        )
    WHERE authority_collection_value = '*OBJINF';
```

Note

Depending on how many IFS objects you have, this may take some time to run. You may wish to modify the starting path name to be something other than '/'.

CHAPTER 10

Tips for Securing the IFS and Avoiding Malware

How one secures the Integrated File System (IFS) remains a mystery to many organizations even though it's been a part of the operating system since V3R6 and is used extensively. The goal of this chapter is to demystify the security aspects of the IFS and to help you make progress in securing it and avoiding malware.

IFS security is a mash-up of IBM i, UNIX, and PC settings. It was originally architected to allow UNIX applications to be ported to what was iSeries at the time. Much of the behavior reflects that, including the names of the data authorities (*R, *W, *X), the fact that the system uses the UID and GID of the profiles rather than the profile name to determine the process's authority, and the fact that the IFS ignores both adopted authority and the Owner parameter in the user profile. (The Owner parameter transfers the ownership of created objects to the user's group profile.) But the fact is, under the covers, IFS objects are IBM i objects, so the object authorities apply (*OBJMGT, *OBJEXIST, *OBJALT, and *OBJREF). Also, the same authority-checking algorithm applies whether you're checking an object in a library or an object in a directory. Auditing (logging) of IFS objects is accomplished via the audit journal rather than syslog. Finally, you can set attributes on IFS objects that are enforced by your workstation, such as Read-only and check-in/check-out.

I explain this to say that on the surface I understand why people are confused, but you need to get past this and realize it's just not that difficult! I've already provided several examples of securing directories in chapter 9. In this chapter, I want to quickly discuss IFS authorities and then focus on reducing the risk of malware infection.

IFS Authorities

Let's start with definitions of each of the authorities:

- *R (Read) authority is what you'd expect. You need *R authority to be able to read the contents of a file. *R also allows you to list the contents of a directory.

- *X (Execute) authority allows you to traverse (go through) one directory to get to the next directory. For example, to reach /home/carol, I need *X authority to both root ('/') and /home.

- *W (Write) authority allows you update an object as well as add an object to a directory.

Mapping IBM i authorities into these authorities, we get:

- *USE = *RX data authorities, object authorities *NONE

- *CHANGE = *RWX data authorities, object authorities *NONE

- *ALL = *RWX data authorities along with object authorities *OBJMGT, *OBJEXIST, *OBJALTER, and *OBJREF

I'm very purposefully pointing out the object authorities here because, while many organizations realize they need to set data authorities, I often see them forgetting—or not realizing—they must also set the object authorities (which goes back to my point that, under the covers, IFS objects are IBM i objects, so all authorities apply to them, not just the data authorities). See Figure 10.1 for an example.

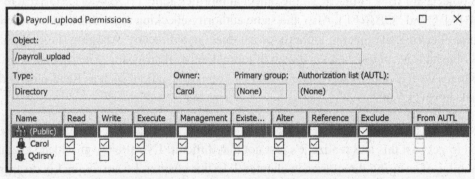

Figure 10.1: Both data authorities and object authorities need to be set for IFS objects.

The reason we need to be concerned about the authority to objects in the IFS is because of the type of data that's often stored (transactions associated with banks or third-party service providers, images containing HIPAA or other personally identifiable information, website configuration files and images to name a few types of data). That, and the risk of that data being downloaded or not available due to malware. Malware no longer just encrypts data. Prior to encrypting the data, malware often downloads (exfiltrates) the data. Then the attackers threaten to post it if you don't pay the ransomware.

Malware affects IBM i in two ways. One is the method that's been around for many, many years. A file or document is infected with malware and then uploaded to the system to be stored in the IFS. This method doesn't affect IBM i itself, but the next time that object is accessed, the user's workstation is typically infected. However, this is not the method that most organizations are concerned about today. And to be honest, they shouldn't be. Most of these infections are caught by a desktop or firewall antivirus solution. The next method poses a much greater risk, both from the chance of occurrence as well as the damage that can occur.

Malware, specifically ransomware, has literally destroyed some organizations, and when it didn't cause the business to go under, it cost many organizations millions of dollars. Organizations have found that some cyber insurance providers cover their malware infection and some don't. The threat is real, so let's determine how you can reduce that risk of infection in the first place.

File Shares

Ransomware infects a user's workstation, and then it starts to spread around the network. How, exactly, does that happen? It doesn't FTP itself or establish an ODBC connection. No, it walks through a workstation and then starts walking through all of the workstation's mapped drives, including any drive mapped to IBM i. How does one establish a mapped drive to IBM i? Via a file share. Every file share defined on IBM i is a potential point of entry for malware. (I've had clients that were infected with malware variants other than ransomware.) Want to reduce your risk of IBM i being infected with ransomware or other malware? First, do *not* share root ('/'). Sharing root shares your *entire system*, including the operating system. Eliminate all file shares not in use, reduce shares defined as Read/Write to be Read-only if possible, and then for the remaining shares, secure the object associated with the share. I worked with a client on this and, after a bit of investigation, realized that of the 10 shares originally defined, they only needed one. They deleted the nine shares not used (including a Read/Write share to root) and secured the directory so that it can be accessed only by the handful of users needing to use it. Risk level went from the potential of having the entire system infected to only being able to be infected if one of the handful of profiles with authority to the directory had their workstation infected, and then the damage would be confined to that one path. Risk *significantly* reduced!

Determining the risk level is fairly easy. Until IBM i 7.5, all shares can be used by any profile on the system; therefore, the risk is a combination of the type of share (Read-only or Read/Write) and the authority on the object shared. I say "object shared" because I've seen more than just a directory shared. A couple of organizations that I've worked with have actually shared a database file in a library?! If a user connects with a Read/Write share but is excluded from the shared object, the malware will have zero impact. However, if the user with the infected workstation connects using *ALLOBJ, a Read/Write share allows the data to be exfiltrated prior to being encrypted. Therefore, your risk of malware infection is minimized when you reduce the shares to only those needed, make them Read-only whenever possible, and restrict access to the object being shared to only those whose job responsibilities require it.

Note

The very important (and very cool) IBM i 7.5 enhancements to IFS security are discussed later in this chapter.

Steps to Reducing the Risk

You can take three steps to greatly reduce the risk of devastating malware/ransomware infections.

Step #1: Examine who is using the file shares and eliminate ones that are no longer in use.

To see the list of file shares defined on the partition, launch New Nav, click on the File folder icon, and choose File Shares, as shown in Figure 10.2. This view lists the shares, the attribute (Read-only or Read/Write), the pathname of the object shared, the number of users currently attached to the share, and an indication of whether the object associated with the share actually exists. I can't tell you the number of systems I've examined where one or more of the shared objects no longer exists. While they don't pose a security risk, they are unnecessary clutter. If the object doesn't exist, delete the share!

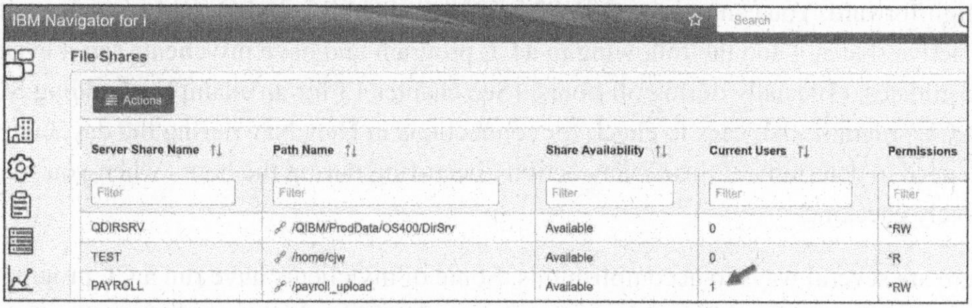

Server Share Name ↑↓	Path Name ↑↓	Share Availability ↑↓	Current Users ↑↓	Permissions
Filter	Filter	Filter	Filter	Filter
QDIRSRV	/QIBM/ProdData/OS400/DirSrv	Available	0	*RW
TEST	/home/cjw	Available	0	*R
PAYROLL	/payroll_upload	Available	1	*RW

Figure 10.2: The File Share category in New Nav shows the number of connected users.

While you're in New Nav, you can see the list of users currently attached to the share. Simply click on the share, right-click, and choose Properties. Scroll down to see the list of Sessions (that is, the list of currently attached users). This method works great while you're at work, but how do you know when a file share is in use when you're not?

If you have IBM i 7.4 or later, the easiest way to determine which profiles are using file shares is to start Authority Collection on each of the paths that are currently shared. Here's an example:

```
CHGAUTCOL OBJ('/payroll_upload') AUTCOLVAL(*OBJINF)
```

Then start the collection if you haven't done so previously.

```
STRAUTCOL TYPE(*OBJAUTCOL)
```

Once enough time has passed that you know the file shares should have been used, run the following:

```
SELECT check_timestamp,
       authorization_name,
       job_name,
       path_name
```

```
FROM qsys2.authority_collection_fsobj
WHERE job_name like 'QZLSFILE%'
        AND path_name LIKE '/payroll_upload%';
```

To determine whether a file share is in use with IBM i 7.3 and earlier is not as straightforward. You can use the QSYS2.SERVER_SHARE_INFO IBM i Service to find the active shares. I add the following to a CL program and have my clients run it every five minutes, especially during off hours. (See chapter 13 for an example of adding SQL to a CL program.) It's easy to check for connections in New Nav during the day, but you need to determine if there's any activity occurring during the hours when you're not actively checking.

There are several ways to accomplish this. Some of my clients have run a CL program that generates a spooled file of the active shares. But I like this example from Scott Forstie:

Create this table first:

```
CREATE TABLE your_lib.shares AS
            (SELECT CURRENT TIMESTAMP AS date,
                    server_share_name,
                    current_connections,
                    text_description
                    FROM qsys2.server_share_info
                    WHERE share_type = 'FILE'
                        AND current_connections <> 0)
            WITH NO DATA;
```

Then run this CL program every five minutes:

```
PGM
RUNSQL SQL('INSERT +
 INTO YOUR_LIB.SHARES  +
 (SELECT CURRENT TIMESTAMP AS DATE,    +
        SERVER_SHARE_NAME. +
        CURRENT_CONNECTIONS, +
        TEXT_DESCRIPTION    +
```

```
       FROM QSYS2.SERVER_SHARE_INFO                        +
       WHERE SHARE_TYPE = ''FILE'' AND                     +
          CURRENT_CONNECTIONS <> 0) ')                     +
                      COMMIT(*NONE) NAMING(*SQL)
   ENDPGM
```

You can then view the results to see which shares are active:

```
select * from your_lib.shares;
```

The challenge is if you find that shares are being used during off hours and it's not obvious by looking at the contents of the directory which profiles are using it. If you have *JOBDTA or *JOBBAS specified in QAUDLVL, you can use the JS audit journal entries to discover which profile is entering the system using the NetServer (that is, via a file share).

Note

If you do not already have *JOBDTA or *JOBBAS in QAUDLVL, do not add it without first considering the impact. These values will log the start, stop, release, and hold of *every* job on the system. On many systems, this could significantly increase the number of audit journal entries generated.

In case you're not at IBM i 7.5 or haven't installed the TR containing the JS audit journal table function, I'll use Copy Audit Journal Entry (CPYAUDJRNE).

```
CPYAUDJRNE ENTTYP(JS) JRNRCV(*CURCHAIN),  F4 to specify start and end times.
STRSQL
SELECT JSTSTP, JSJOB, JSUSER, JSNBR, JSUSPF
FROM qtemp/qauditjs
WHERE JSJOB LIKE 'QZLSFILE%'
```

Timestamp	Job name	User name	Job number	User profile
2022-03-08-16.23.38.788928	QZLSFILE	QUSER	26,005	CAROL
2022-03-09-09.33.47.036096	QZLSFILE	QUSER	26,005	CAROL

Figure 10.3: Use the information from the JS audit journal entry to determine who is connecting via a file share.

You can use the output from this SQL to correlate the access with the timestamp in the your_lib.shares file to determine which file share is in use.

For shares you've identified that are no longer needed, right-click on the share name and choose Stop Sharing to delete it.

Shares to Root ('/')

All shares to root should be eliminated. As I've said previously, a Read/Write share to root puts your entire system, including the operating system, at risk of being infected with malware. Even if the share is defined as Read-only, there's still risk. That's because much of the ransomware and other malware exfiltrates (downloads) the data first. So even though the data wouldn't be able to be encrypted (Read-only shares do not allow objects to be modified), it could still be downloaded. Shares should be defined at the subdirectory where the work is to be accomplished, *never* at the root level.

Many organizations share root out of convenience. Now is the time to adjust that thinking and be more targeted as to what is shared. But before you just stop sharing root, you probably want to find out who's using the share. I've found that many people have used the share to root once (perhaps at the behest of the Help Desk), checked the "Reconnect at signon" box when the share was first established, and are now forever mapping to root. It's likely those users don't need to map to anything, or if they do, it's much lower in the directory structure. Developers and administrators also often have a perpetual connection to root (again, out of convenience). While I understand the convenience aspect, I cannot advocate putting your system at that level of risk.

I recommend creating a share to your /home directory and perhaps some other "working" directory. Then, when you need to access that information, access the share via the Windows Explorer command line rather than a perpetual mapped drive. This ensures that the connection is not perpetual while still providing access to the path being shared via Windows Explorer.

You can connect via the partition's IP address or partition name. The format of the command is \\server\share. See Figure 10.4. Notice that there is no mapped drive! Simply close the window to end the access.

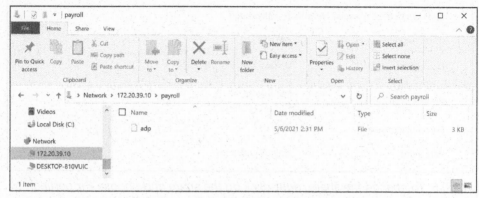

Figure 10.4: Access a share via the Windows Explorer command line.

Step #2: Reduce Read/Write shares to Read-only where possible.

Now that you've eliminated shares to root and shares that aren't being used, examine any remaining shares defined as Read/Write to determine if they can be reduced to Read-only. While the data shared can still be downloaded, the objects shared won't be able to be modified, thus eliminating the possibility of them being encrypted.

To change the share permissions (Read-only or Read/Write), right-click and choose Properties. See Figure 10.5. You will need to investigate what the share is being used for before you can change this attribute. If users are simply downloading from the directory and not uploading, you should be able to change the attribute. If there's one upload occurring from someone's desktop, however, it must remain as a Read/Write share.

PAYROLL Properties	
General	
IBM i Support for Windows Network Neighborhood	
Share name:	PAYROLL
Description:	Upload payroll to processor
Access:	Read/Write ⌄
Encryption required:	NO ⌄
Path name:	/payroll_upload 🔗

Figure 10.5: To change the share, right-click on the share and choose Properties.

While we're looking at Figure 10.4, I'd like to point out a new field. New Nav introduces the "Encryption required" attribute, which is provided as part of the SMB3 support added in IBM i 7.3. Enabling this attribute means that the connection is encrypted. This is a powerful attribute that should be implemented if you're using SMB3 (which many organizations either have already implemented or are planning to).

Step #3: Set the appropriate permissions to IBM-supplied directories.

At this point, you've removed unnecessary shares, probably had to remap some users from a share to root to some other share defined closer to the objects being accessed, and set shares to Read-only where possible. For all remaining shares, the next step is to review the permissions on the object being shared with the goal of reducing access to only those users with a job responsibility that requires access.

I gave several examples of reducing authorities to directories in chapter 9, so I'm not going to repeat those. What I haven't discussed is reducing the authority to several system-shipped directories. Let's start with '/' and /QOpenSys. Both directories ship with the equivalent of *PUBLIC *ALL, specifically, DTAAUT(*RWX) and OBJAUT(*ALL). That's not OK for two reasons. You can't control what's being created into these directories, and everything created under them (including subdirectories) inherits this wide-open authority, so the issue just propagates.

The best practice setting for these two directories is the equivalent of *USE authority: DTAAUT(*RX) OBJAUT(*NONE). Don't forget to set the object authorities! However, to ensure you're not going to break something, before you reduce both directories' *PUBLIC authority setting, you'll want to check to see if any processes are routinely creating objects into them. I've encountered processes that create a temporary object into root and then delete it. An example of this is an email feature of an application. Back in the day, people didn't realize they should use their own directory, and some of them did everything under root. Some applications are still written that way. If you secure '/' then this process will probably break.

To check for objects being created into root, we look at the Creation of Objects (CO) audit journal entries. (To generate these entries, you must have *CREATE specified in QAUDLVL.) The following looks for CO entries generated in the last 14 days. Obviously, you can change this to match the timeframe that matches your requirements.

```
SELECT entry_timestamp,
       user_name,
       qualified_job_name,
       program_library,
       program_name,
       path_name
FROM TABLE (
         systools.audit_journal_co(STARTING_TIMESTAMP => CURRENT
            TIMESTAMP - 14 DAYS)
     )
WHERE path_name NOT LIKE '/%/%';
```

Once you've reviewed the list of actions and changed any processes to create the object into an application-created directory, set the *PUBLIC authority of root to DTAAUT(*RX) OBJAUT(*NONE) using either the Change Authority (CHGAUT) command or Permissions in the Integrated File System feature of IBM i Access Client Solutions (ACS).

You'll use the same CO entries to look for processes creating objects into '/QOpenSys'.

The following SQL statement lists objects that have been created directly into the '/QOpenSys' directory:

```
SELECT entry_timestamp,
       user_name,
       qualified_job_name,
       program_library,
       program_name,
       path_name
    FROM TABLE (
            systools.audit_journal_co(STARTING_TIMESTAMP => CURRENT
                TIMESTAMP - 14 DAYS)
        )
    WHERE path_name LIKE '/QOpenSys%'
        AND path_name NOT LIKE '/QOpenSys/%/%';
```

Finally, I encourage you to consider reducing the *PUBLIC authority of /home. The recommended setting for /home is DTAAUT(*X) OBJAUT(*NONE). This is a different recommendation than I've made in the past. I heard Margaret Fenlon from IBM Rochester speak, and she made this recommendation, pointing out that many organizations create a /home directory for at least some if not all of their users. My previous recommendation of DTAAUT(*RX) allowed anyone to list the contents of the /home directory, thus seeing at least a partial list of user profiles. I have since proved this theory during our DXR Security penetration-testing engagements. Using SSH or ACS's Integrated File System feature to name just two methods, it's very easy to list the contents of the /home directory, no special authorities required.

IBM i NetServer Settings

The NetServer is the server on IBM i that makes the mapped drive connections. Two attributes of the NetServer itself can make the system either more or less vulnerable.

- Announcements: If the NetServer doesn't "announce" itself, then it and the file shares cannot randomly be discovered on the network. Users will need to know the name of the partition and share to be able to map a drive.

- Guest Profiles: A guest profile assigned to the NetServer allows someone to connect using the profile named in the Guest profile attribute. This allows users without an

IBM i profile to connect to the system. If a Guest profile has been assigned, you will want to remove it if it's not purposely in use (a rare occurrence).

Checking for Announcements

When the NetServer "announces," it broadcasts the names of all of the file shares defined on the system. (The exception is when the share name contains a $ at the end.) To check whether the NetServer is announcing, do the following:

Launch Navigator for i and click on the icon shown in Figure 10.6 then Servers > TCP/IP Servers.

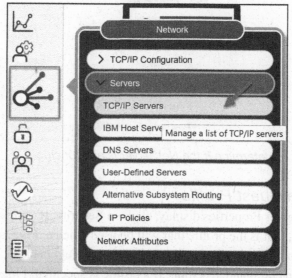

Figure 10.6: Click on the highlighted icon > Servers > TCP/IP Servers.

When the window of servers is displayed, right-click on IBM i NetServer and choose Properties. Click on Advanced to determine if the NetServer is announcing. See Figure 10.7. If Send browse announcements is Yes, then NetServer is announcing and share names will be broadcast and discoverable by anyone in the network. Click on Expand Next Start to see the fields at the bottom of the display. Uncheck the Send browse announcements box. Click on Collapse Next Start. The change will take effect after you stop and restart the server.

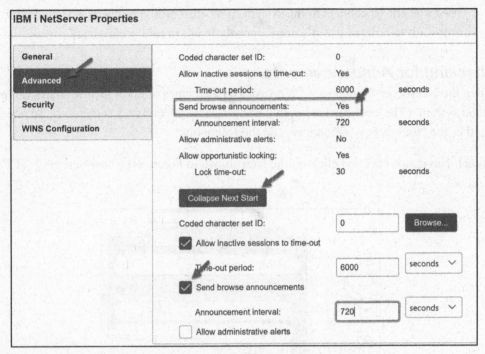

Figure 10.7: Check to determine if the NetServer is announcing.

Checking for a Guest Profile

While on the NetServer Properties display, click on Security. If you see a name in the Guest user ID field, that is the profile that will be used when a drive is mapped, and no user ID and password are provided. In Figure 10.8, that field is blank, indicating no Guest profile. This is the recommended setting. If a profile is specified, I highly recommend that you create a profile for anyone using the Guest access and remap them using their own user profile. (If the Guest profile is in use, you'll see that profile's name as the profile connected in the Session information when you examine who's using a file share.)

To remove a Guest profile, click on Expand Next Start, blank out the profile name, and click Save. Stop and restart the NetServer to have this change take effect.

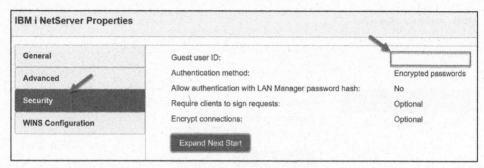

Figure 10.8: Check for a Guest user ID.

Reducing the Risk: Exported Mountpoints

Another way IBM i could get infected with malware is via an exported mountpoint using an NFS mount. A mount is used to connect to another server. The Export File System (EXPORTFS) command is used on System_A to define the path to be "exported." But what it really means is that System_B can do a mount, and the path from A appears on B as if it resides on B. In this scenario, your IBM i (System_A) is vulnerable to malware should System_B become infected.

To view mounts that have been defined, go to Navigator for i > Network > Servers > TCP/IP Servers. Click on NFS and then right-click to choose Mounts. If no mounts have been defined, this option will be grayed out. As with file shares, if the mounts are no longer needed, they should be removed.

Reducing the Risk with IBM i 7.5 Enhancements

IBM has responded to the threat of malware infection with significant enhancements in IBM i 7.5.

Control Access to the NetServer

IBM i 7.5 provides significant enhancements for protecting access to the IFS! The first one I'll describe is for the NetServer itself. A new attribute has been added to the NetServer Properties that allows you to specify an authorization list associated with the NetServer. See Figure 10.9.

IBM i NetServer Properties

General	Guest user ID:
	Authentication method:
Advanced	Allow authentication with LAN Manager password hash:
Security	Require clients to sign requests:
WINS Configuration	Encrypt connections:
	Authorization List:

General	Guest user ID:
	Authentication method:	Encrypted passwords
Advanced	Allow authentication with LAN Manager password hash:	No
Security	Require clients to sign requests:	Optional
WINS Configuration	Encrypt connections:	Optional
	Authorization List:	

Collapse Next Start

Guest user ID: [   ]

Authentication method: [Encrypted passwords ⌄]

☐ Allow authentication with LAN Manager password hash

Require clients to sign requests: [Optional ⌄]

Encrypt connections: [Optional ⌄]

Authorization List: [|]

Reset to Current   Save

Figure 10.9: Control access to the NetServer via an authorization list.

Similar to how the QPWFSERVER authorization list doesn't secure any objects but restricts access to the /QSYS.LIB file system via interfaces such as the Integrated File System feature of ACS and Windows Explorer, the authorization list specified for the NetServer doesn't secure an object either. Rather, *USE or greater authority to the list allows use of the NetServer. Unlike the QPWFSERVER authorization list, no authorization lists associated with this feature are shipped; therefore, to take advantage of this new control, create an authorization list specifically for this purpose (e.g., NETSERVER).

Note

Please do not use an existing authorization list and overload it with this function, and please add a meaningful description—if not for yourself, for those coming after you who must determine what the authorization list is used for!

```
CRTAUTL AUTL(NETSERVER) TEXT('Control access to NetServer > *USE has
     access')
```

If you haven't yet determined who's using file shares (see previous discussions in this chapter), I'd suggest that you set it to *PUBLIC *USE until you do. (Or set it to *PUBLIC *EXCLUDE and be prepared to have your phone ring when access fails for people and processes!) Once you've determined which profiles require access (that is, are accessing the system via a file share), consider creating a group (perhaps, again NETSERVER and an appropriate text description so you know its purpose), grant the group profile *USE authority to the list, and then set the list to *PUBLIC *EXCLUDE. After that, only members of that group can connect to the system via a file share.

Use of this new attribute will allow you to tightly control which profiles are allowed to access the system via the NetServer—that is, via a file share.

Control Access to a Specific File Share

The addition of this support brings file-share support more in line with the Windows concept of a file share, where you can control who can use the actual share and not have to rely on the users' permission to what's being shared.

This ability is again implemented using an authorization list, and again, it does not secure any object. Unlike the other authorization lists, however, the actual authority granted matters. For both the QPWFSERVER and NetServer authorization lists, a user with *USE or greater has access. It doesn't matter if you've granted a profile *CHANGE or *ALL, users don't have any more access than a profile granted *USE. Not so in this case:

- If a profile has *USE authority to the authorization list associated with a file share, the user will have Read-only access.

- If a profile has *CHANGE (or greater) authority to the authorization list associated with a file share, they will be allowed Read/Write access.

- Access for users with *ALLOBJ special authority acts the same way as it does when accessing any object. When *ALLOBJ is assigned to the user profile, access cannot be denied, and the user will have Read/Write access.

To take advantage of this new function, in New Nav, click on the File Share, and then right-click and choose Properties. See Figure 10.10.

PAYROLL Properties

General
IBM i Support for Windows Network Neighborhood

Share name:	PAYROLL
Description:	Upload payroll to processor
Access:	Read/Write ⌄
Encryption required:	NO ⌄
Authorization List:	SHARE1|
Path name:	/payroll_upload

Figure 10.10: To secure an individual share, assign an authorization list.

Again, I encourage you to create a unique authorization list for each file share for which you intend to restrict access. And, again, I encourage you to use a meaningful naming convention and text description to make very obvious the purpose of the list. For example:

```
CRTAUTL AUTL(SHARE1) TEXT('Secures the PAYROLL share')
```

Then add the users or groups to the list, but in this case, make sure you grant them the appropriate permission corresponding to the access you wish to give them: Read-only (*USE) or Read/Write (*CHANGE).

 Tech Note

The audit journal entry generated when a user attempts to map a drive and doesn't have authority to an authorization list associated with either the NetServer or an individual file share will be a VP entry, not an AF entry.

Tech Note

The QSYS2.SERVER_SHARE_INFO IBM i Service has been updated
in IBM i 7.5 to include the name of the authorization list associated
with the share (if any).

This new and very powerful feature of IBM i 7.5 allows you to create shares that only
administrators should be able to access. This does not, however, give you free rein to
create shares to root! As an administrator, if your workstation is infected and you're
mapped to that share, the entire system may get encrypted since you have *ALLOBJ.
That risk does not go away! And if you say, "That will never happen," let me remind you
of the events of the last few years and then tell me with a straight face that that could
never happen!

Final Recommendations for Reducing Risk in the IFS:
- Restrict who can define new shares or modify existing ones by

   ○ setting the *PUBLIC authority of the Add File Server Share (QZLSADFS) and
   Change File Server Share (QZLSCHFS) APIs to *EXCLUDE. Note: This step
   will have no effect on users with *ALLOBJ.

   ○ limiting the users with *IOSYSCFG special authority. (Users with *IOSYSCFG
   can create shares. Without *IOSYSCFG, one must be the owner of the object to
   create a share for it.)

- Across the organization, review shares that are automatically reconnected when a
  workstation is reconnected or rebooted to ensure the user needs to be connected
  to the share. (This applies to all shares, including Windows shares, not just IBM
  i shares.) With the danger of malware and especially ransomware, automatically
  connecting a user to a drive "just in case" they need it is no longer an option.

- When creating shares, add a $ to the end of the share name. If the NetServer is set
  to broadcast, a $ at the end of the share name will hide it from being discovered.

- Set the IBM-shipped QPWFSERVER authorization list to *PUBLIC *EXCLUDE
  to limit who can see and access the /'QSYS.lib' file system via interfaces such as

ACS's Integrated File System feature, Navigator for i, and Windows Explorer. Note: This does not restrict users' access when running their applications or access via ODBC, FTP, etc.—only the list functions of the interfaces listed.

- Verify that your backups are current, and verify that they are saving what you think they should be saving. Backups are key to recovery should the system (or parts of the system) become infected with malware.

- Educate your users on the current threats of the day, including phishing, smishing, Business Email Compromise (BEC), social engineering, and more.

- Make sure you have an Incident Response Plan. Review it and go through exercises with it regularly to ensure you've accommodated the current threats. For ideas on IBM i considerations you should make in your Incident Response Plan, see chapter 20 in *IBM i Security Administration and Compliance*.

A Green-Screen Method to Manage NetServer Security

Obviously, the purpose of this entire book is to help you use more modern interfaces. But in the interest of getting you to use these updated features of the NetServer as well as for those organizations that limit the use of web interfaces, there's a green-screen menu that you can enable that will allow you to control the NetServer as well as see what file shares have been defined, etc. The menu is GO NETS, but you must first restore it. Instructions for doing so are here:

https://www.ibm.com/support/pages/manage-ibm-i-netserver-without-navigator-go-nets

CHAPTER 11

Implementing Function Usage (Application Administration)

I've written about the Navigator for i feature called Application Administration for many years, but with New Nav it has a new name as well as a new look and feel. I'm a big fan of implementing multiple layers of defense, and Function Usage provides several ways to do just that.

First, the name change. Application Administration may have sounded better, but once you understand the feature, it really has no meaning. Function Usage, while it may not be obvious, at least has a correlation to the CL command Work with Function Usage (WRKFCNUSG), which allows you to manage this feature in the green-screen. I was the leader of the IBM i Security Team (it was actually iSeries at the time) when we delivered this feature, and I remember the discussion on what to call it. Believe it or not, Function Usage was actually the best name! The feature defines whether a profile is allowed to *use* a *function,* where a "function" is something that needs to be controlled but for which there is no object to secure. That's how the name came about.

While the look and feel of the feature in New Nav is totally different, the areas that it controls have not changed. There are still three: the categories in New Navigator for i, the features of ACS, and several actions that take place on IBM i itself. The intent of the first two areas is to allow you to customize the features of New Nav and ACS so that users only see or are allowed to use the features that align with their job responsibilities. The concept is very similar to only presenting the menu options that users are allowed to take, and it's an appropriate application of the security concept of "least privilege access." While I would not recommend this be the only way you limit access to New Nav and ACS features, it's the easiest and it will provide at least some protection. I also recommend customizing your ACS deployments to only include the features you want people to use as well as more generally limiting what people can install on their PCs and removing Admin rights.

To access Function Usage in New Nav, hover over the padlock icon and choose Function Usage as shown in Figure 11.1.

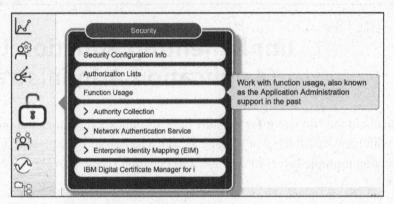

Figure 11.1: Hover over the padlock icon to get to the Function Usage feature.

Controlling Access to New Nav

Let's take a look at how controlling New Nav and ACS is accomplished. One thing I really like about this new version of Function Usage is that it's far easier to control access to the New Nav categories. In Heritage Nav, you couldn't control access at the category level. You had to set the controls at every function under each category. You could copy them from function to function, but that was less than handy. In New Nav, functions have *only* been defined at the category level for Navigator for i, not for the functions under each category.

Tech Note

Word of warning! Function Usage restrictions defined for Heritage Nav *do not* get mapped into New Nav Function Usage settings. You must reapply settings for New Nav yourself! (Settings you've defined for ACS and IBM i remain in place.)

Be aware that no attempt has been made to map whatever current functions you may have restricted in Heritage Nav into the new functions that have been defined for the categories in New Nav. Because of the way features have been categorized, reworked, and deprecated, there was no way to accurately map between Heritage and New Nav categories/features. If IBM had attempted to map the functions, they most assuredly would have missed something or simply gotten it wrong. Controls that you put in place in Heritage Nav *must* be redefined in New Nav. I know numerous organizations that depend on these settings to limit end user access to Navigator for i. Unless you take action, your organization may be allowing unintended access via Navigator for i. (Any restrictions you may have put in place for ACS or the Host (IBM i) functions will remain. This rework only applies to the functions controlling access to Navigator for i.)

The good news is that there's one function ID, QIBM_NAV_ALL_FUNCTION, that allows/disallows access to New Nav, making it very easy to shut off access. To find the functions that allow you to control New Nav, filter the Function ID column using qibm_nav, as shown in Figure 11.2. The entries shown roughly correspond to the icons (categories) along the left side of the display.

Function Usage

≡ Actions

Function ID ↑↓	Function Name ↑↓	Default Usage ↑↓	All Object Indicator ↑↓	Profiles Allowed / Denied ↑↓
qibm_nav	Filter	Filter	Filter	Filter
QIBM_NAV_USERS_GROUPS	USERS AND GROUPS	ALLOWED	USED	NO
QIBM_NAV_FILE_SYSTEM	FILE SYSTEM	ALLOWED	USED	NO
QIBM_NAV_SERVICEABILITY	SERVICEABILITY	DENIED	USED	NO
QIBM_NAV_CUSTOM_CHARTS	CUSTOM CHARTS	ALLOWED	USED	NO
QIBM_NAV_ALL_FUNCTION	USE OF IBM NAVIGATOR FOR i FUNCTIONS	ALLOWED	USED	NO

Figure 11.2: Filter the Function ID column to list the categories defined for New Nav.

To allow or disallow access, click on the function and then right-click and choose Change. I find this display much easier and more intuitive to use than the displays in Heritage Nav. For example, to me, it's much more obvious what "Allowed" and "Denied" mean for the Default authority rather than checking or unchecking the selection as in Heritage Nav. In the example shown in Figure 11.3, I'm changing the Default access from Allowed to Denied. Once I press OK, unless the profile has *ALLOBJ, the user will be prevented from using New Nav. I could even take this one step further and also change the *ALLOBJ special authority setting from Used to Not Used and then specify the ADMIN group profile in the Profile(s) box and click Add under Access Allowed, then OK. Now the only users allowed to use New Nav are the members of the ADMIN group profile.

Tech Note

IBM will set the default access for QIBM_NAV_ALL_FUNCTION to Denied when the New Nav PTFs are first applied. If you have Allowed or Denied users, those settings will remain. If you wish to allow all users access, you will need to change the Default access back to Allowed. If you don't leave the default access as Denied, I recommend you take this opportunity to customize access and not allow all users access to all features of New Nav.

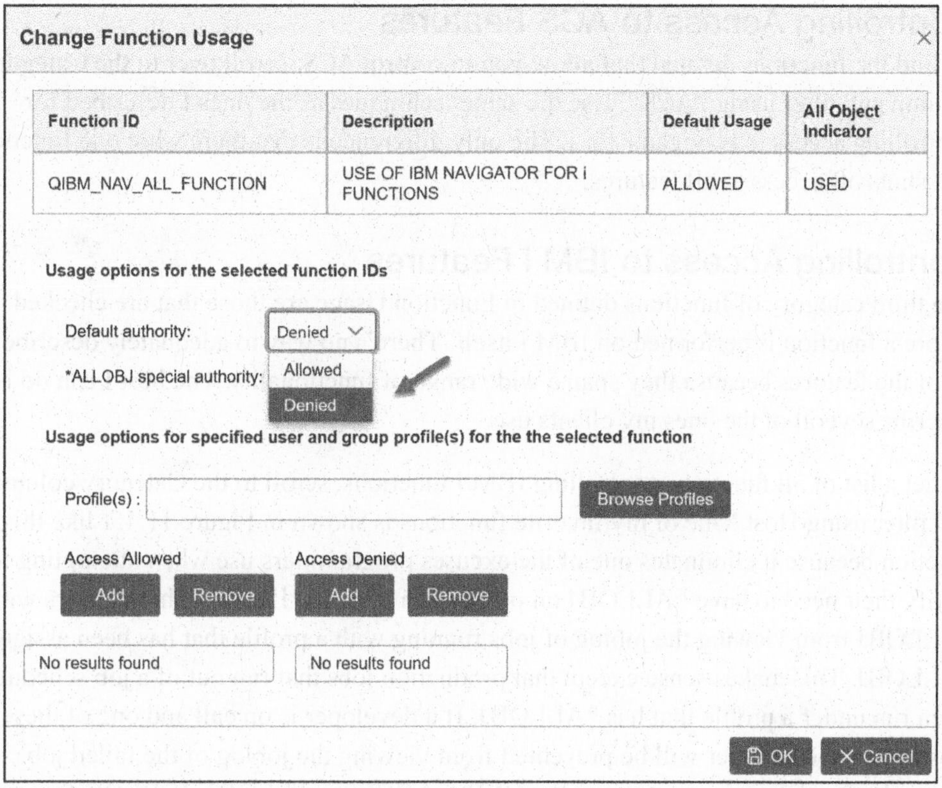

Change Function Usage   ✕

Function ID	Description	Default Usage	All Object Indicator
QIBM_NAV_ALL_FUNCTION	USE OF IBM NAVIGATOR FOR i FUNCTIONS	ALLOWED	USED

Usage options for the selected function IDs

Default authority: | Denied ∨ |

*ALLOBJ special authority: Allowed

Denied

Usage options for specified user and group profile(s) for the the selected function

Profile(s) : [   ]   Browse Profiles

Access Allowed   Access Denied

Add   Remove   Add   Remove

| No results found | | No results found |

💾 OK   ✕ Cancel

Figure 11.3: You can easily change the default settings or allow/deny access for specific users or groups.

Another term that caused some confusion in Heritage Nav was "Customize," meaning that you want to allow or deny specific users or groups as I've just discussed. Rather than Customize, you'll now see a column entitled "Profiles Allowed/Denied" with the value of either NO or YES. If NO, well, hopefully it's obvious. No users or groups have been allowed or denied specific access to this function. If YES, well then…they have!

Controlling Access to ACS Features

To find the functions defined that allow you to control ACS, scroll over to the Category column and filter using "ACS." Use the same techniques as the ones I described for controlling access to Navigator for i. The only difference is that there's not one function that shuts off access to all features.

Controlling Access to IBM i Features

The third category of functions defined in Function Usage are those that are checked before a function is performed on IBM i itself. There's no way to adequately describe all of the features because they span a wide range of functionality. The best I can do is describe several of the ones my clients use.

To get a list of all functions controlling IBM i functions, scroll to the Category column and filter using Host. One of my favorite functions is shown in Figure 11.4. I like this function because it eliminates one of the excuses programmers use when attempting to justify their need to have *ALLOBJ on production systems. IBM i prohibits users without *ALLOBJ from viewing the joblog of jobs running with a profile that has been assigned *ALLOBJ. This makes sense except that production jobs that run out of a job scheduler often run under a profile that has *ALLOBJ. If a developer is on call and one of these jobs fails, the developer will be prevented from viewing the joblog of the failed job… unless they've been given access to the QIBM_ACCESS_ALLOBJ_JOBLOG function and they have *JOBCTL special authority. It's rare that developers on call don't have *JOBCTL; that, combined with having access to this function, provides them with the ability to continue to debug these jobs, without having *ALLOBJ themselves. Simply specify the developer's group profile in the Profile(s) field and click Add under the Access Allowed column.

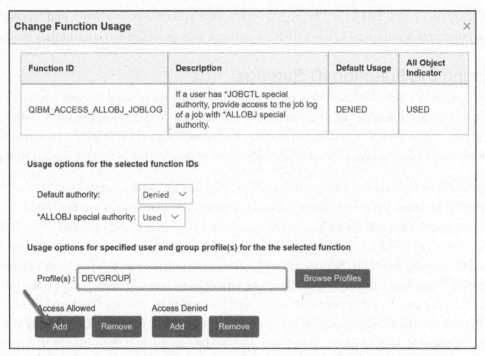

Function ID	Description	Default Usage	All Object Indicator
QIBM_ACCESS_ALLOBJ_JOBLOG	If a user has *JOBCTL special authority, provide access to the job log of a job with *ALLOBJ special authority.	DENIED	USED

Usage options for the selected function IDs

Default authority: Denied ∨

*ALLOBJ special authority: Used ∨

Usage options for specified user and group profile(s) for the the selected function

Profile(s) : DEVGROUP| Browse Profiles

Access Allowed   Access Denied

Add   Remove   Add   Remove

*Figure 11.4: Allow individuals and groups with *JOBCTL to access *ALLOBJ joblogs.*

My other three faves control access to the system via DDM/DRDA (QIBM_DB_
DDMDRDA function), ODBC (QIBM_DB_ZDA), and FTP (QIBM_QTMF* functions).
Think of these functions as on/off switches for DDM/DRDA, ODBC, and FTP. Either
users can access the system via these protocols or they can't. There's no filtering on the
object they're trying to access or controlling by time of day or originating IP address.
If you need to be that granular with your access controls or you need to log the details
of what's being accessed or the SQL being used on the request, then you need to use an
exit program. But if you're simply trying to shut off access via these protocols, these
functions do the trick. You have the same ability to deny access by default, use or not use
*ALLOBJ to allow access, and list specific users/groups to allow or deny access. I've had
clients that knew exactly which profiles should be using ODBC, for example. They used
the QIBM_DB_ZDA function, changed the default access to Denied, allowed *ALLOBJ

(because users with *ALLOBJ are tightly controlled in their environment), and listed the two other profiles allowed to use ODBC. For them, this provided the control they needed.

Listing the Function ID Settings

If you want to have a different way of viewing these settings or need to print a report or send it to a spreadsheet or file, you have a few options. You can use the Work with Function Usage (WRKFCNUSG) or Display Function Usage (DSPFCNUSG) commands. But the output is display or spooled file only and the spooled file is not the easiest to read.

When you're viewing the settings in New Nav, you can export the entries you're currently viewing. Choose Actions > Export. Finally, you can always use the IBM i Service to get a list and then click on the results and send that to a spreadsheet. The IBM i Service is QSYS2.FUNCTION_INFO, and you can certainly write your own SQL to list the details using Run SQL Scripts. But if you have the entries you want but can't export them all (New Nav can only export the rows you're viewing, which may not be the full list of entries), go to the upper right corner and click on SQL. What's displayed is the SQL used to select the entries you're viewing. You can either run that SQL directly if you have configured ACS to do so, or you can copy and paste the SQL into Run SQL Scripts.

Using the Audit Journal to Detect Access

As I've explained in earlier chapters, when any function ID is changed (either default access or you allow a profile or group access), the operating system starts to generate a GR audit journal entry whenever one of these function IDs is checked. When are they checked? When I sign in to New Nav, all of the function IDs associated with New Nav are checked to see which categories I'm allowed to use. When I make an ODBC connection, the QIBM_DB_ZDA function is checked to determine if my profile is allowed to make the connection. Each check results in a GR audit journal entry. These entries give you the ability to determine who's accessing the system via FTP, ODBC, and DDM/DRDA, which is incredibly helpful when trying to determine how to secure objects. See chapter 9 for a more-detailed explanation of using the GR audit journal entries.

You Need to Do More Than Just Control New Nav and ACS to Secure Your Data

I started this chapter saying that Function Usage was one way to implement multiple layers of defense. Please make sure that it's not the *only* defense you take to secure your system. Using Function Usage and other forms of limiting access to Navigator for i and ACS functions is basically the same as implementing "menu security" in a green-screen environment. Assuming that limiting users' access to the user interface is protection enough is turning a blind eye to the fact that there are *many* ways to access IBM i data, not just Navigator for i and ACS. If you want to ensure your data is secure, you *must* secure your data with object-level security!

CHAPTER 12

Securing the Connection to IBM i

Up to this point, my focus has been on making sure you have the ability to use modern interfaces to discover your IBM i security settings. This chapter switches focus to the actual connection being made to the system and the additional layers of defense you can add to these connections as part of your security scheme.

TCP/IP Servers

I'm not going to discuss the security considerations of each TCP/IP server; I did that in *IBM i Security Administration and Compliance, Third Edition*. What I want to encourage you to do is review the servers that you have autostarting and determine if that's the right setting. If you aren't using it, change the autostart value. For example, there are known exposures with the *REXEC server. Hopefully, it's not in use, and therefore, I'd make sure the autostart value is *NO.

The easiest way I know to display (and change) the servers using autostart is to use New Nav. Click on the icon shown in Figure 12.1, then TCP/IP Configuration, then TCP/IP Configuration Properties.

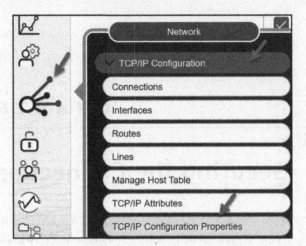

Figure 12.1: Use New Nav to display the TCP/IP Configuration Properties, including the autostart value.

Figure 12.2 shows a portion of the window that's displayed when you click on Servers to Start. To change the autostart attribute, simply check or uncheck the box in front of the server. It couldn't be easier than that.

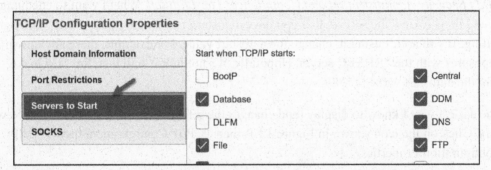

Figure 12.2: Click on Servers to Start to display or change the autostart value of the servers.

Exit Points

I alluded to exit points when I described using Function Usage to control access to FTP, ODBC, and DDM/DRDA. An exit point is a point defined by the operating system where a user-written program can be called.

Several types of exit points have been defined throughout IBM i. One is where the exit program is passed a predefined set of information and, based on that information, the exit program can send back to the operating system an indication as to whether the process should continue or fail.

Another type of exit is informational—that is, at the time the exit program is called, the operating system passes a predefined set of information; however, the exit has no say as to whether the action will take place. For example, there are exit points that have been defined when a profile is created, restored, and deleted. The exit program is passed the name of the profile and the action being taken. This provides the opportunity for the exit program to take action on its own, such as creating the user's /home directory or adding them to the system distribution directory when the profile is created and then deleting those when the profile is deleted. But regardless of what the exit program does, the action on the profile will occur.

Exit points that have the ability to stop an action have been around for many years, and several vendors provide software that puts a user interface to these exits, allowing you to control access to many (but not all) connections to the system. Because there aren't exits for every method of accessing the system, you will always hear me emphasizing the need to implement object-level security because it's *always* in place. However, using exit points can provide an additional layer of defense if you need more "situational" access controls—for example, if you want to allow an ODBC connection only from a specific IP address and block all others. Or only allow FTP during business hours.

The other reason to use exit points is for the logging opportunities they provide. I've described how you can use the GR audit journal entries to determine when users are entering the system via FTP, ODBC, or DDM, but that's about all the information you get. The audit journal doesn't provide the name of the object being accessed or the SQL being run; however, an exit program can log that information, and you can have a more-detailed idea of what's happening on your system by reviewing the logs associated with the transactions flowing through the exit program. Most organizations only use exit point software for its logging capabilities, but exit programs can be used to add an additional layer of security if you use the rules and block access. Some organizations have made exit programs an integral part of their security program.

To see the exit programs defined on the system, along with the programs assigned to those exit points, you can use Work with Registration Information (WRKREGINF), but the output is only to display or a spooled file. If you want to send it to a spreadsheet or to filter it differently than the command allows, you can use the QSYS2.EXIT_POINT_ INFO to list the exit points available. From that view, you can see which exits have programs assigned and then use QSYS2.EXIT_PROGRAM_INFO to list the programs.

Controlling Who Can Use SSH

One of the servers I am going to spend a bit of time on is Secure Shell (SSH) because it's become widely used and SSH clients are readily available. If you're not controlling what can be installed on your users' desktops, an SSH client such as PuTTY can be download, installed, and in use in just minutes.

One of the popular features of most SSH clients is the file-transfer capability. The secure connection capabilities of SSH clients provide an alternative to unencrypted FTP connections. This feature may not seem like a security exposure and shouldn't be if you've implemented object-level security. But if you're like many IBM i organizations that haven't taken this step or rely on exit-point technologies to secure your critical files, you've got an issue. (Note: IBM has not provided an exit point for the SSH daemon, and attempting to control access via the Sockets exit is tenuous at best.) SSH is a secure tunnel over which several different types of processes can flow. The fact that it's multi-featured is one reason why I believe that IBM hasn't provided an exit point specifically for SSH and why it's often difficult to know how to block it, even at the firewall level.

If you're not using SSH in your organization, make sure the autostart value is *NO. If you are using SSH, follow the instructions below to limit who can use it and the directories in which users can operate.

When you think about who should be able to use SSH, it's typically limited to a handful of people, often just administrators. Controlling which profiles are allowed to connect via SSH is actually quite simple. It can be accomplished by adding one or more directives to the configuration file associated with the SSH daemon. The configuration file can be found at this path:

```
/QOpenSys/QIBM/UserData/SC1/OpenSSH/etc/sshd_config
```

The directives available for controlling access are DenyUsers, AllowUsers, DenyGroups, and AllowGroups. Regardless of the order in which they're defined in the config file, they are evaluated in the order I've listed. You don't have to specify values for all of these directives. (In fact, it doesn't work if you do!) If you only want the members of one group (e.g., GRPSSH) to be able to use SSH, you only need to specify AllowGroups grpssh. Everyone who is not a member of GRPSSH is denied access.

What seems to work well for my clients is to create a group specifically for SSH use. If a user needs to use SSH, put them in this group. The group can be specified as either their Group profile or as one of their Supplement group profiles. Do not overload this group— that is, do not use it for any purpose other than to control SSH. That way, there's much less chance that you'll have to exclude users in the configuration file—in other words, use the DenyUsers directive.

If you happen to have the situation where you have a group in which some but not all members of the group need SSH access, you can then go ahead and use the DenyUsers directive, specifying the names of the profiles that shouldn't be allowed to use SSH. See Figure 12.3. Now, only members of the GRPSSH and SYSADMS groups will be allowed use of SSH, except for John, Joe, and Sam. All other users are also denied, just like John, Joe, and Sam are.

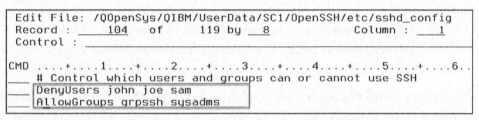

Figure 12.3: Allow or deny SSH access to groups or individuals.

You'll want to take note of these items:

- *Do not* use both AllowUsers and AllowGroups. You can use one or the other but not both.

- The profile and group names must be specified in lowercase! The directive itself is not case-sensitive, but the values are and, counter to what one might think, it's expecting the values to be in lowercase.

- When specifying multiple profiles (or groups), separate each with a blank.

- You must end and restart the server to have your configuration changes take effect.

Other Best-Practice Settings

You may also want to change some of the default settings in your SSH configuration file. For example, I recommend that you do not let QSECOFR use SSH. (QSECOFR is a well-known profile. If someone is going to try to access your system, that's a profile they know exists on all IBM i systems like root exists on all UNIX/Linux systems.) To disallow QSECOFR login, set PermitRootLogin to No.

Other configuration options to set:

- Your organization (likely your lawyers) may require all logins to display a banner stating access is for management-approved uses only. Specify the path to the banner (Banner /your pathname) where the banner is located.

- Only allow the more secure SSH2 protocol (Protocol 2).

- Use Session idle time-out (ClientAliveInterval 300).

- Session keep-alive number is the number of times users get a warning message that their session is about to time-out. If your time-out value is 300 and you set the keep-alive to 5, users will get a warning every 5 minutes, and if the session is idle, it will time-out after 25 minutes. It's a bit like the QINACTITV and QINACTMSGQ system values. For SSH, it's recommended that you just time-out the inactive session and don't have a keep-alive (ClientAliveCountMax 0).

- Set a max number of sign-on attempts (MaxAuthTries). Match your QMAXSIGN system value, typically 3-5.

- Consider using public/private keys for authentication and disallowing the use of passwords on the connection. Here's a link to the support page describing how to configure this: https://www.ibm.com/support/pages/configuring-ibm-i-ssh-sftp-and-scp-clients-use-public-key-authentication

- Disallow host-based authentication, which is different from and even less secure than user ID/password authentication (HostbasedAuthentication no).

Finally, consider configuring chroot. chroot is a UNIX/Linux method of setting a process's root directory to restrict what the process can access. You may also see it referred to as a "container" or "jail." Containers are often used when implementing automated SSH and SFTP processes. You know that I'm all for multiple layers of defense, and I do appreciate using chroot to provide at least a speedbump in the road to limit what users of SSH can access. But, just as prisoners can tunnel under prison walls or find other means of escape, users can escape the confinements of chroot. I'm not saying not to use it; please do. Just don't depend on it as your single method of securing SSH access. Also, if you're set up to allow a specific group, don't forget to add this group profile to the profiles you've set up in your chroot configuration. For more information on chroot and IBM i, see this support page: https://www.ibm.com/support/pages/using-chroot-ibm-i-restrict-ssh-sftp-and-scp-specific-directories

Discovering Who's Using SSH

Before you limit which profiles can use SSH, you may want to determine who's already using it so you can either allow the access or make the conscious choice to prevent it. There's no specific audit journal entry type for SSH access, but I've discovered that you can determine SSH access by examining either the GS entries (generated by specifying either *SECURITY or *SECSCKD in QAUDLVL) or the JS entries (generated by specifying *JOBDTA or *JOBBAS in QAUDLVL). I'm providing an example using the GS entries since it's more likely you already have the GS entries. (More organizations have *SECURITY as a value in QAUDLVL than *JOBDTA or *JOBBAS.)

First, retrieve the GS entries:

```
CPYAUDJRNE ENTTYP(GS) JRNRCV(*CURCHAIN)
```

Then get a list of entries including the timestamp, user, and IP address fields:

```
SELECT GSTSTP, GSUSPF, GSRADR FROM QTEMP/QAUDITGS WHERE GSJOB = 'SSHD'
```

Whether you use the GS or JS entries, you'll notice that there are multiple entries for a single connection. (The best way to understand this is to make an SSH connection yourself and look at the audit entries generated.) Unfortunately, the timestamp, user, and IP address are really the only useful information the audit journal provides for SSH, whether you are looking at the JS or GS entries. Obviously, actions taken, such as the creation or deletion of objects, will generate their respective audit journal entries, but examining the CD (Command) audit journal entries will not yield the commands entered via SSH. The only way to log the activity that occurs via SSH is to enable syslog. Enabling syslog is not what you'd call straightforward on IBM i. Here's a link to an IBM Support document that describes the process: https://www.ibm.com/support/pages/syslog-syslogd-pase-ibm-i

SNMP

The other server I need to mention is Simple Network Management Protocol, better known as SNMP. This is the TCP/IP protocol that allows you to manage devices throughout your network, of which IBM i may be one. The problem with this protocol is that intruders can use it to map out your network, and the first two versions of this protocol make that quite easy to do. IBM i 7.5 builds on the enhancements in IBM i 7.4 to only allow SNMPv3. If you use SNMP in your network or you specifically want to prevent the SNMP agent from running on your system, see https://www.ibm.com/docs/en/i/7.5?topic=snmp-controlling-access for more details and recommendations.

Encrypted Sessions

I can't emphasize enough the need to encrypt all sessions—not just communications out of your network, but internal communications as well. Why, you ask? Because if malware or an intruder makes its way into your network, all data (including user IDs and passwords flowing around your network in cleartext) will be read, especially the user IDs and passwords. They will be skimmed and used to gain access to servers around your network, harvest the data on those servers, and/or plant additional malware. Encrypting internal communications eliminates the chance of user IDs and passwords from being skimmed and data from being stolen in this manner.

How does one encrypt communications to your IBM i? Most servers are registered in Digital Certificate Manager (DCM). Web applications must first be configured to use SSL/TLS, and then they're registered in DCM. You can define your IBM i to be a Certificate Authority (CA)—that is, the entity that creates digital certificates—but most organizations choose to get a certificate from a well-known CA or have an internal CA so that the certificates will be trusted by browsers. (If you choose to have your IBM i be your CA, you'll have to download its CA certificate into the trust list of all users' browsers to ensure the connections are encrypted—that is, use https. If not, some browsers will revert the connection to http when they don't trust the issuing CA.)

If you've never considered configuring your connections to IBM i to be encrypted, using your IBM i as the CA is a good place to start. All of the software you need is already provided by the operating system and likely already installed. In other words, it will take no additional funds for you to give this a try. You can continue using your IBM i as a CA, but if you decide not to, you already know how to get things configured. You simply import the certificate into DCM and follow the same steps as you did to configure the servers when your IBM i was the CA.

DCM got a facelift a while ago, but many people missed that message. So with New Nav, the link it provides is the link to the new DCM interface. See Figure 12.4.

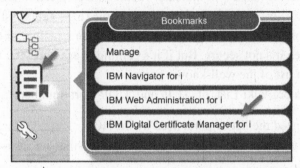

Figure 12.4: An easy way to launch DCM is through New Nav Bookmarks.

Unfortunately, IBM's documentation hasn't kept up with the new interface. That said, the link below provides very good step-by-step instructions for creating a CA on IBM i, requesting and importing a certificate from a well-known CA, and assigning it to servers and more. While the screenshots are the old interface, the terminology and flow in the new DCM is the same as the old, so you should be able to follow along. If you haven't used DCM, I encourage you to use this resource to get familiar with this important part of configuring encrypted sessions: https://www.ibm.com/support/pages/digital-certificate-manager-dcm-frequently-asked-questions-and-common-tasks

Ensuring All Communications Are Encrypted

It's easy to determine whether my connection to IBM i is encrypted. If I'm using Access Client Solutions (ACS) to establish a Telnet session, all I have to do is look in the lower right corner of the session to see the port used, an open or closed padlock, and encryption strength if the connection is secure. For ODBC, I simply look for the job name to be QZDASSINIT (SS meaning secure) rather than QZDASOINIT (where SO is open or not encrypted). But if I'm an administrator and I want to prove to myself or am required to prove to an auditor that all connections are secure, how might I do that?

NETSTAT

One way to look at all connections is to use the Work with TCP/IP Network Status (WRKTCPSTS) command, aka NETSTAT. Choosing to look at the IPv4 and IPv6 connections will show you the established connections and which server they're connected to. The server name will indicate whether the connection is secure, typically by adding either -s or -ssl to the end of the server name (e.g., Telnet-ssl). The port used is also an indication of whether the connection is secure. For example, if the Telnet session is using port 23, then it's not secure. But if it's coming in via port 992, the connection is encrypted. Here's a list of the well-known ports:
https://en.wikipedia.org/wiki/List_of_TCP_and_UDP_port_numbers

In addition, you'll need the list of ports used by the ACS:
https://www.ibm.com/support/pages/tcpip-ports-required-ibm-i-access-and-related-functions

By analyzing the output of NETSTAT, you can determine whether there are currently any unsecured connections established to your IBM i. The problem with NETSTAT is that it's a point in time; it's accurate only for the time at which you ran the command. Other connections may be established in the middle of the night, for example.

The Audit Journal

To have a complete analysis of your connections, you'll need to utilize the audit journal. You'll need to add two values to the QAUDLVL system value: *NETTELSVR to audit Telnet connections and *NETSCK to get all other IP connections. (If you want to analyze UDP connections, you'll need to add *NETUDP.) Once you've added these values, all connections will be logged. (Note that these values may generate a significant number of audit journal entries, so once your analysis is completed you may want to remove these additional values from QAUDLVL.)

To analyze the connections, you'll need to gather the SK audit journal entries. The SK entries aren't (yet) available as a service, so we'll use CPYAUDJRNE to get the information:

```
CPYAUDJRNE ENTTYP(SK) JRNRCV(*CURCHAIN) FROMTIME(startdate starttime)
    TOTIME(enddate endtime)
```

There are many subtypes within the SK audit journal entry (for the full list, see the *IBM i Security Reference* manual, chapter 9), but the subtype we're looking for is 'A', meaning that the connection has been accepted. So right away, I'm going to use the following SQL statement to filter the SK entries to just look for the accepted connections.

```
SELECT *
    FROM qtemp/qauditsk
    WHERE SKTYPE = 'A'
```

Even with this filter, you're still likely to have a lot of entries. At this point, your next step depends on why you're examining these entries. If you think you've gotten all connections secured, you may want to specifically look for connections coming in over unsecured ports. The following SQL lists the ports that the connections should be using; anything coming in over a different port will be listed. (Note: This is not a complete list of secure ports!)

```
SELECT *
    FROM qtemp/qauditsk
    WHERE SKTYPE = 'A'
          AND SKLPRT NOT IN ('22', '443', '992')
```

If you are just starting out with this project, you'll probably want to be more selective in the entries. For example, if you want to ensure all Telnet sessions are encrypted, you can use an SQL that will only include cleartext Telnet sessions (that is, connections coming in over port 23).

```
SELECT *
    FROM qtemp/qauditsk
    WHERE SKTYPE = 'A'
          AND SKLPRT = '23'
```

Now that you've selected the audit entries, how do you read/make sense of the information in the audit journal entry? For most audit journal entry types, I find the job name, user, and number helpful as well as the program and program library. But in this case, these fields are worthless. That's because these entries are generated before the user's job has started. See Figure 12.5.

```
75  SELECT skjob,
76         skuser,
77         sknbr,
78         skpgm,
79         skpgmlib,
80         sklprt,
81         skradr
82     FROM qtemp.qauditsk
83     WHERE SKTYPE = 'A'
84          AND SKLPRT = '23';
```

Job name	User name	Job number	Program name	Program library	Local port	Remote IP address
SKJOB	SKUSER	SKNBR	SKPGM	SKPGMLIB	SKLPRT	SKRADR
TNACCEPTTA	SK	0	*NONE	*OMITTED	23	10.20.39.2

Figure 12.5: SK entries are generated before the user's job starts, so traditional fields are of little use.

Likewise, the User profile field that typically contains the name of the current user is also worthless in this audit journal entry as it will always contain the value *NONE. So what is helpful about this entry? You'll want to focus on these two fields:

- SKLPRT: Local port

- SKRADR: Remote IP address

To decipher where the connection is coming from, you'll have to do a reverse DNS lookup using the remote IP address. You may also find the timestamp (SKTSTP) field helpful if the connections are coming from remote servers and you have to look through scheduled jobs to find the incoming task.

Helpful Hints

As you start to play around with the SK entries, you may want to force a few entries to understand how to better read and understand what you're seeing. (That's what I always do when I start using an audit journal entry type that I'm not familiar with.) To force the entry, remember that SK entries log new connections; therefore, it's not sufficient to simply log off your Telnet session and log back on. That will not generate an SK entry. You must close and reinitiate the session to get an SK entry generated.

Note that the *NETCMN value was reworked in IBM i 7.3 such that it no longer logs accepts and connects. If you have *NETCMN specified in QAUDLVL and think you're going to get the audit journal entries I've been describing, you won't. As I said earlier, you must specify *NETTELSVR and *NETSCK (and NETUDP if you want to analyze your UDP connections) in the QAUDLVL system value. It may take a bit of investigation, but analyzing the SK audit journal entries will help you know whether all connections are secure (encrypted) or not.

Ensure All Connections Are Using Strong Encryption

The other consideration for encryption is the strength of the algorithms in use. The system values that control the strength of encryption on the system are the QSSL* system values. I describe the three values and how they work together in chapters 3 and 10 of *IBM i Security Administration and Compliance, Third Edition*. IBM i 7.4 changed the default settings such that the default protocols implemented no longer enable weak protocols. Unfortunately, I've seen organizations blindly set the QSSLPCL system value back to include weak protocols (which in turn enables weak encryption algorithms) just because they want to make certain they don't run into problems. Please resist the temptation to do that! You can easily determine whether weak protocols are in use on your system. The IBM Support page shown below provides instructions for going into Service Tools and enabling counters to count the number and type (SSLv3, TLS1.0, TLS1.1, etc.) of encrypted sessions. The instructions are buried toward the end of this page (https://www.ibm.com/support/pages/security-bulletin-vulnerability-sslv3-affects-ibm-i-cve-2014-3566), so here they are for your convenience:

1. Access System Service Tools by using SST. Type STRSST and sign on with your Service Tools ID and then take the following menu options:

2. 1 - Start a service tool.

3. 4 - Display/Alter/Dump.

4. 1 - Display/Alter storage.

5. 2 - Licensed Internal Code (LIC) data.

6. 14 - Advanced analysis. (You must page down to see this option.)

7. Page down until you find the SSLCONFIG option. Type 1 (Select) next to the option and press Enter. You are now on the Specify Advanced Analysis Options window. The command shows as SSLCONFIG.

You now have several actions you can take. To see the entire list, enter -h and press Enter to display the options available.

For example, to start tracking the connections, issue the following option:

```
-sslConnectionCounts:enable
```

The count starts immediately. No need to stop/restart anything or to IPL.

Once the counter has been enabled for a period of time, go back into SST following the instructions above and type the following to display the results as shown in Figure 12.6.

```
-sslConnectionCounts:display
```

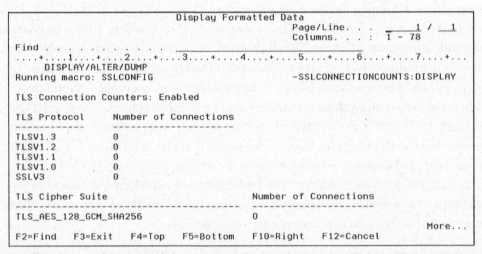

Figure 12.6: Use the SSLCONFIG macro in SST to determine if weak protocols are being used.

Note that the counts will be reset with every IPL, and you'll have to go back in and re-enable the counts.

To stop the counters, issue the following:

```
-sslConnectionCounts:disable
```

To reset the counts without having to IPL, issue the following:

```
-sslConnectionCounts:reset
```

If you find that weak protocols or ciphers are in use, this link provides the instructions for running a trace to determine which job(s) used them: https://www.ibm.com/support/pages/how-determine-ssltls-protocol-and-cipher-suite-used-each-active-system-tls-connection-ibm-i

There's really no excuse for blindly enabling weak ciphers by adding weak protocols back into QSSLPCL when it's so easy to determine whether they're required. I recommend that you go through this process to ensure your encrypted sessions are using strong encryption.

Be aware that some vendors, such as those supplying secure file transfer or database encryption, may use their own encryption configuration and not rely on the QSSL* system values. If you have software that provides any type of encryption, check with the vendor to ensure their product uses strong encryption and that the version you have installed has that support.

Securing New Nav

Finally, you'll want to make sure that New Nav is using a secure connection: that is, https (not http). Several years ago, IBM stopped shipping a self-signed certificate with its browser interfaces due to the number of browsers that were either downgrading the connection from https to http or rejecting them altogether when a self-signed certificate was in use. IBM Support has provided instructions for enabling Navigator for i to use https. While the instructions have been upgraded to say that they can be used for New Nav, some of the instructions only reference Heritage Nav. Make sure that you are enabling SSL/TLS for the ADMIN1 HTTP admin server job, which is the server for New Nav. The examples also only show using a self-signed certificate. I recommend that if you have access to a well-known CA, you use a certificate issued by that CA rather than a self-signed certificate so the certificate won't be rejected or downgraded by browsers.
https://www.ibm.com/support/pages/enabling-tls-ibm-navigator-i

CHAPTER 13

Automating Your Analysis

I understand that I've been describing doing analysis in real time but that many of you need to run the same report or perform the same analysis over and over again. And many of you need to have reports scheduled regularly for audit purposes. This chapter will discuss some of the options you have for automating your analysis.

Run SQL Scripts

Of course, by now you should realize that you don't have to re-create your SQL. You can use the Save function in Run SQL Scripts to save your work. What I suggest you do is put all of the SQL that you need to run regularly into a separate Run SQL Script file; then run each statement one at a time. When the results appear, right-click on the results and choose the Save Results... option to generate your report as an .xlsx, .csv, or whatever format meets your requirements. (You must first enable the Save option. See chapter 1 for instructions.)

SQL in a CL Program

While running established SQL statements regularly may work for you, some may need or want to run the SQL from a scheduled job. Unfortunately, both the regular and advanced job scheduler take only CL commands, not SQL. So how do you schedule SQL? One way you can accomplish it is to put your SQL in a CL program. You have two options for running SQL from a CL program: Run SQL (RUNSQL) and Run SQL Statement (RUNSQLSTM). To use RUNSQLSTM, put your SQL into a source physical file or a file in the IFS and then use RUNSQLSTM in your CL program to run the SQL defined in that source file. Here's an example: https://www.ibm.com/support/pages/sample-cl-program-run-sql-scripts-using-runsqlstm

However, most people use RUNSQL, and that's the command I'll use for my example. The tricky part of adding SQL to a CL program is that you can't use the SELECT statement, so you have to do a bit of sleight of hand to get the SELECT accomplished.

```
PGM

              MONMSG      MSGID(CPF0000) EXEC(GOTO CMDLBL(RETURN))


/* DELETE PREVIOUS OVERRIDES TO ENSURE RPTS HAVE THE CORRECT NAME  */
              DLTOVR      FILE(*ALL) LVL(*)
              MONMSG      MSGID(CPF0000)


              DLTF        FILE(QTEMP/DFTPWD)
              MONMSG      MSGID(CPF2105)
              RUNSQL      SQL('CREATE TABLE QTEMP.DFTPWD   AS     +
        (SELECT AUTHORIZATION_NAME, LAST_USED_TIMESTAMP, STATUS, +
              SPECIAL_AUTHORITIES, GROUP_PROFILE_NAME, +
              SUPPLEMENTAL_GROUP_LIST, TEXT_DESCRIPTION FROM    +
              QSYS2.USER_INFO   +
         WHERE USER_DEFAULT_PASSWORD = ''YES'' +
         ORDER BY STATUS) +
                          WITH DATA') COMMIT(*NONE) NAMING(*SQL)
              MONMSG      MSGID(SQL9010) EXEC(GOTO CMDLBL(RETURN))


              OVRPRTF     FILE(QPQUPRFIL) MAXRCDS(*NOMAX) +
                          SPLFNAME(DFTPWDS) OVRSCOPE(*CALLLVL)


              RUNQRY      QRYFILE((QTEMP/DFTPWD)) OUTTYPE(*PRINTER) +
                          FORMSIZE(*RUNOPT 378)
              MONMSG      MSGID(SQL9010) EXEC(GOTO CMDLBL(RETURN))
 RETURN:
              DLTOVR      FILE(*ALL) LVL(*)
              MONMSG      MSGID(CPF0000)
ENDPGM
```

A few notes regarding this program:

- First, this program is provided as is: no warranties, use at your own risk, and whatever words I need to use to make sure I'm not liable in case it fails or doesn't work for you!

- Now for some info that will actually be helpful…

    ○ All literals have to be qualified with two single quotes. Notice my WHERE clause; the *YES is surrounded with two sets of single quotes (those are not double quotes). Note: This issue will bite you if you have just copied your SQL from Run SQL Scripts because that interface uses one single quote to qualify literals.

    ○ I use a naming convention of *SQL (NAMING(*SQL)) so I can use the period (.) rather than a slash (/) to name objects—for example, QSYS2.USER_INFO.

    ○ I specify COMMIT(*NONE) so I don't have to worry about uncommitted transactions being rolled back.

    ○ While this specific example works without it, in other CL programs running SQL, I've had to specifically set my CCSID to the language on my system to have the report correctly display the information.

For what I was working on when I wrote this program, I needed to create a spooled file (thus my use of the RUNQRY command). But you may want to send the contents of the file to a stream file and then download it to Excel. Or maybe you generate the spooled file as I did and then PDF it and email it off the system. My intent in providing this example is not to provide you with a total solution but to get you thinking about how you might make this work in your environment, using the utilities you already have. In addition, many other examples of adding SQL to a CL program exist on the Internet; you can learn from those. If you want a more-thorough explanation of RUNSQL, you can find it here: https://www.ibm.com/support/knowledgecenter/ssw_ibm_i_74/sqlp/rbafyrunsql.htm

Using Administration Runtime Expert (ARE)

My final example for this chapter is truly one of those hidden gems of IBM i. Administration Runtime Expert (ARE) is a no-charge IBM i Licensed Program Product that allows you to automate various tasks such as PTF distribution, which is especially helpful when you're managing multiple partitions. But in the context of checking security configuration, it's also very helpful and not just when you have multiple partitions; it's also useful when managing one partition. You can check system value settings, network attributes, TCP/IP configuration settings, user profile configurations, as well as object authorities against what you've defined as your baseline settings. You can also "fix" settings. It has its own scheduler, so you can schedule these checks to run on a regular basis and be sent a report of the results. Finally, my favorite feature: You can schedule SQL statements. So if one of the predefined categories' (known as plugins in ARE) attributes aren't exactly what you want to check, you can use the SQL that you've been developing throughout this book.

Let's take a closer look at ARE. Once you have installed the prerequisite products, PTFs, and ARE itself (5733-ARE), you'll have to start the servers that process ARE:

```
QSYS/STRTCPSVR SERVER(*HTTP) HTTPSVR(IBMARE)
```

Open a web browser and access ARE via http://system_name:12401/are. This launches the Deployment Editor, where you'll create a "template," and within that template you'll define the checks you want to make. See Figure 13.1.

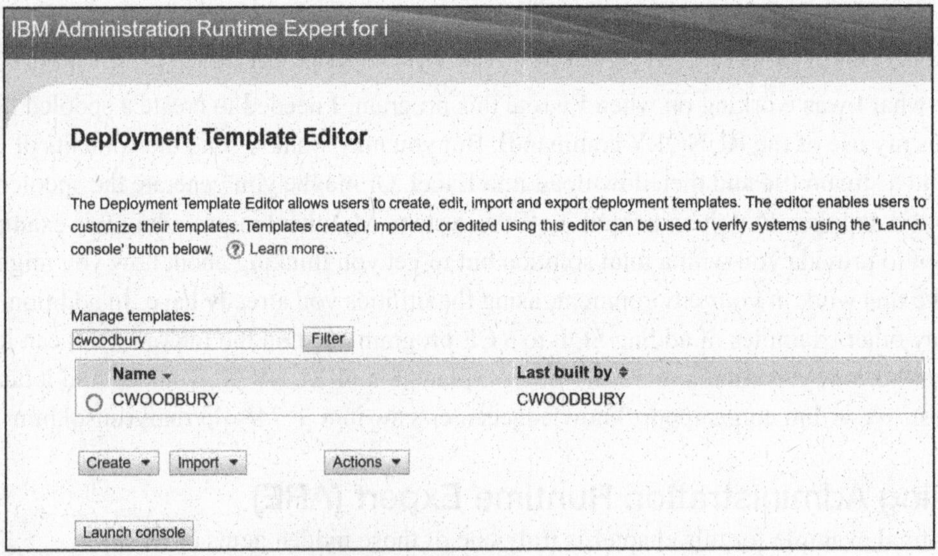

Figure 13.1: Deployment Template Editor in ARE.

Choose Create and name your template. Figure 13.2 shows the categories available. Open each category to see the plugins available. Click on Edit (see Figure 13.3) to customize the plugin and add it to your template. This is now known to ARE as a "collection." (Yes, I agree that the ARE terminology could use a bit of help.)

Figure 13.2: Open each category to see what plugins are available.

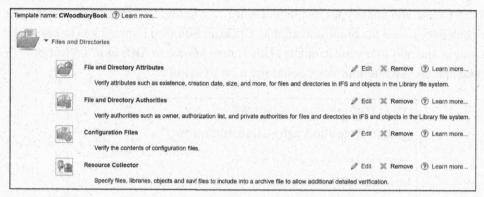

Figure 13.3: Click on Edit to customize a plugin and add the collection to your template.

Once you've edited one or more plugins (that is, created one or more collections), click on Build template on the Plugin Selection display. Building the template puts it in the format ARE needs so it can be used to verify a system. That is, the values in the template are compared to the values on the system against which the template is being run. If you make changes to the template but don't rebuild it, the changes won't be picked up when it's used to verify the system.

Once you've built the template, go back to the Deployment Template Editor and click on Launch console. See Figure 13.4. From here you can select the template, specify the systems you want to verify, schedule the verification to run at a specific time (ARE has its own job scheduler), use the Runtime properties to specify that the reports should be emailed, and more.

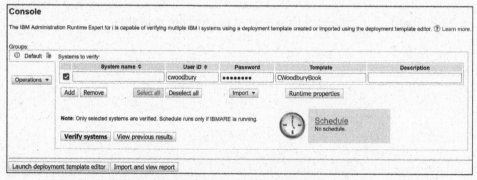

Figure 13.4: Use the Console to Verify (check) the template.

When you're first starting to use ARE, I suggest that you create a template, play around with the ARE features (including using the SQL Query Writer for your customized SQL statements), build the template, and then launch the console and verify a system. If you're checking object authorities, change the authority of one or more objects and make sure you understand how to read the report that's generated when you verify the system. Same with user profile and system value changes. Then, I'd create a template for each type of information being checked. For example, one template for system values, another for user profiles, etc. This way, you can check the template whenever you wish and schedule it to be checked on whatever schedule makes sense for your organization. If you put everything you're checking in one template, then everything will be checked whenever you verify a system. While that may meet your needs, my clients usually need some parts of the system checked more often than others, so templates need to be defined with more granularity.

More hints for using ARE:

- Be descriptive with the names of both your templates as well as the collections. That way, you can tell the purpose of the template at a glance and don't have to go in and edit it to determine what it does.

- I've already said this, but I'm going to say it again: Don't overload your template with collections that don't go together; in other words, don't add multiple collections to the same template when it doesn't make sense for the collections to be verified at the same time. For example, if your organization needs to verify system values once a week but needs to check the configuration of profiles with *ALLOBJ every day, don't put them in the same template.

- Understand that when you create a File and Directory Attribute collection, it takes a snapshot of the contents of the library or directory you've included. It does not automatically add new objects to the collection after the collection has been defined.

- Avoid including the same libraries or directories in multiple templates. That can lead to inaccurate or confusing results.

- Read the ARE documentation. I realize that no one likes to read documentation and you're going to just try to figure it out on your own. But trust me on this one: Reading the documentation will save you time and frustration. Here's a link to all of the documentation available for ARE: https://www.ibm.com/support/pages/ibm-administration-runtime-expert-i

CHAPTER 14

A Little Bit of Everything

This chapter is a nod to everyone who has ADHD. I'm going to constantly change topics, and none of them are going to fit together! It's the place where I'm putting every topic that I wanted to discuss but wasn't long enough to have its own chapter.

Other IBM i 7.5 Enhancements to Be Aware Of

I've already described some of the enhancements and changes in this release, but there are several more I want to point out.

- It's been best practice to change the sign-on messages CPF1120 - User xxx does not exist and CPF1107 - Password not correct to be the same text and to remove the message IDs so people with ill intent don't know which one they've gotten wrong. IBM i 7.5 eliminates the need to change these messages. IBM has changed the text for CPF1120 to be User xxx does not exist or Password not correct for user profile. CPF1107 is no longer issued. New Nav also issues a generic sign-on failed message. Yay! This is a great enhancement because as many times as I've recommended people do this, they rarely do!

- List functions (both commands and SQL Services), such as those that list the contents of a library or directory or objects secured with an authorization list, have been changed to require that the user has some authority to the object. In other words, if the user has *EXCLUDE to the object, it won't display in the list or be returned via a retrieve function. This change also ensures that what is returned by commands is the same list as is available via the SQL Services. (In some cases, an SQL Service returned objects the user didn't have authority to but the command did not.) Getting these list functions to return only what a user is authorized to is an important security change/enhancement. If a user doesn't have authority to an object, they absolutely have no reason to know it exists and definitely shouldn't be seeing information or statistics. This change can be overridden by changing the default setting or allowing some users access to the QIBM_LIST_ALL_OBJS or QIBM_LIST_ALL_OBJS_SQL functions (using the Function Usage feature in New Nav or the Work with Function Usage (WRKFCNUSG) command), but I highly recommend that you *not* change the default setting unless something truly breaks; and even then, perhaps the better (more secure) action would be to change the process rather than these functions.

- Another important change is similar to the previous bullet: Objects under /home will not be listed if users are excluded from them. Prior to IBM i 7.5, if you have *R to /home, its contents will be listed, which is usually at least a partial list of user profiles on the system. Now, if you set individuals' /home/profile_name directory to DTAAUT(*EXCLUDE) OBJAUT(*NONE), the home/profile_name directory won't be listed using interfaces such as ls in QSH, and the profile names won't be exposed. (Don't forget to set the Object authorities to *NONE; if you don't, the *PUBLIC authority will still have some authority, and it will continue to be listed!) Prior to upgrading to 7.5, you can eliminate this exposure by removing *R authority from /home.

- The Service tool IDs 11111111 and 22222222 are removed, which I think is great because I know of no one who used them and they were consistently left with default passwords.

- In much the same way that you can lock security-related system values from being changed, you can now lock password exit programs. In other words, by using service tools you can determine whether password-related system values can be removed.

- The QRETSVRSEC system value is now obsolete. This makes sense because everyone changed it from the default of 0 to 1 anyway. In fact, many things didn't work if you didn't change it, so getting rid of it makes sense.

- RSTUSRPRF *ALL no longer has to be performed in restricted state.

- The default *PUBLIC authority setting when creating a journal and journal receiver is now *EXCLUDE. Again, a great change. (This should serve as a reminder to check the *PUBLIC authority of QAUDJRN and the attached journal receivers, all of which should be *PUBLIC *EXCLUDE.)

- A new feature of the IBM i procedure SET_SERVER_SBS_ROUTING allows you to route users into specific subsystems when the connection is coming in from a secure (encrypted) database—such as ODBC—(QZDASSINIT) or file server (QPWFSERVSS) connection. Routing users to specific subsystems isn't new, but prior to this you couldn't route them when these connections were encrypted.

- When you read the Memo to Users (MTU), you'll notice a whole bunch of programs, files, job descriptions, and other object types in several IBM-supplied libraries whose *PUBLIC authority has been changed from *ALL or *CHANGE to *USE. I consider this a cleanup rather than a major change. These objects should have been shipping as *USE and somehow slipped through with another authority. It's good to see IBM set these authorities correctly. None of the changes should cause compatibility issues, but you'll want to read through the list to make sure.

- Many other changes are occurring in this release. If you are not in the habit of reading the MTU, *do not* skip this important step, and read it thoroughly *before* you upgrade! And if you're skipping a release (for example, upgrading from IBM i 7.3 to 7.5), make sure you read the MTU for *both* releases—the one you're upgrading to as well as the one you're skipping.

Table Functions That Help Keep Your System Current

One of my absolute favorite table functions that I want to make sure you're aware of is SYSTOOLS.GROUP_PTF_CURRENCY. When run, it does a "phone home" to IBM to get the latest group PTFs and then performs a comparison to determine whether the system you're running the table function on has the current group PTFs installed or there's a newer group PTF available. I'm not sure how you determine this information any other way. I'm guessing it's available on some IBM Support website, but good luck finding it. Another table function to be aware of, SYSTOOLS.FIRMWARE_ CURRENCY, performs a "phone home" and comparison to determine if your system's firmware is current.

These two simple and easy-to-use functions help you ensure that your system stays current. Use them!

Using the Integrated Security Tools: SECTOOLS

While I've talked about New Nav and using SQL to get information about IBM i security, I realize that some of you are more comfortable in the green-screen environment or you run in a very strict environment where you can only use a green-screen (yes, those exist!), so I want to make sure you're aware of the CL command-based security tools that come with the operating system. Be aware: They are basic. And what you see is what you get; zero customization is available. But if you want or need something basic, this is it. And these tools come with the operating system.

You access these tools by typing GO SECTOOLS from a command line. The SECTOOLS menu lists numerous utilities and reports that will help you make an assessment of your IBM i security configuration. See Figure 14.1.

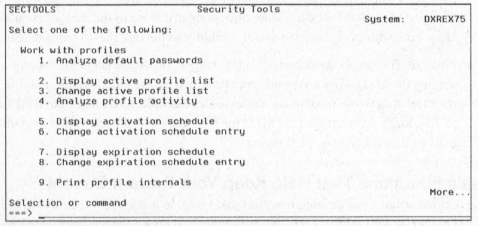

```
SECTOOLS                      Security Tools
                                                  System:    DXREX75
Select one of the following:

  Work with profiles
    1. Analyze default passwords

    2. Display active profile list
    3. Change active profile list
    4. Analyze profile activity

    5. Display activation schedule
    6. Change activation schedule entry

    7. Display expiration schedule
    8. Change expiration schedule entry

    9. Print profile internals
                                                          More...
Selection or command
===> _
```

Figure 14.1: Type GO SECTOOLS to get to this menu.

Option 1 is simply the Analyze Default Password (ANZDFTPWD) command, which produces a report listing profiles with a default password (a password that is the same as the user profile name). I'm going to skip the rest of the menu options on this page for the moment and scroll down to the second page of the menu. See Figure 14.2.

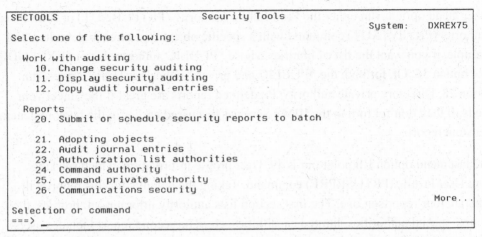

```
SECTOOLS                        Security Tools
                                                     System:    DXREX75
Select one of the following:

  Work with auditing
     10. Change security auditing
     11. Display security auditing
     12. Copy audit journal entries

  Reports
     20. Submit or schedule security reports to batch

     21. Adopting objects
     22. Audit journal entries
     23. Authorization list authorities
     24. Command authority
     25. Command private authority
     26. Communications security
                                                              More...
Selection or command
===>
```

Figure 14.2: Auditing commands and Reports are on the second page of the menu.

I use menu option 11, Display security auditing, to determine what action auditing (if any) has been configured. I also use it to find the naming convention of the audit journal receivers. I can then run the Work with Journal Receivers (WRKJRNRCV) command to find out how many days' worth of audit journal receivers are on the system—in other words, how many days of audit information are available without having to restore journal receivers from a backup. If auditing has not yet been configured on the system, use menu option 10, Change security auditing, to do the initial setup. It will create the audit journal as well as create and attach the journal receiver and change the auditing system values for you.

Menu option 21 starts the Reports section. These options run commands that generate a variety of reports containing security-relevant information, including adopted authority (option 21), job and output queues (option 44), and trigger programs (option 47), to name a few. Menu option 46, System security attributes, provides a report of the current and recommended settings for the security-relevant system values and network attributes. I recommend that you run this report to get a quick view of these important settings. It also provides the recommended setting for each value. While I don't necessarily agree with all of the recommendations, it does provide a place to start. For my recommendations as well as considerations you'll want to make prior to changing a system value, see chapter 3 of *IBM i Security Administration and Compliance, Third Edition.*

Other menu options run either the Print Public Authority (PRTPUBAUT) or Print Private Authority (PRTPVTAUT) command with a specific object type already defaulted. For example, if you want the list of libraries whose *PUBLIC authority is not *EXCLUDE, take option 36. Or, for both the *PUBLIC and private authorities to directories, run option 28, Directory private authority. Predefined reports are great if they meet your needs. If they don't, I turn to the IBM i Services discussed earlier in the book to generate a custom report.

The last menu option I'll point out is 49, User profile information, which runs the Print User Profile (PRTUSRPRF) command. Taking the defaults for this report will generate four reports in one. The first section lists authority information: profiles, their groups, special authorities, limited capabilities, etc. The second report includes users' initial program, initial menu, job description, etc. The third report includes password information, such as the profile status, number of invalid sign-on attempts, whether the profile has a password, password expiration interval, password last-change date, and more. The fourth and final section can be ignored unless you're down-leveling the system's password level (which, hopefully, rarely happens). Again, this is a simple way to generate one report containing a lot of information about all profiles on the system. But if you want information in a different format that can be customized and/or sent to a spreadsheet, you'll want to go to the QSYS2.USER_INFO IBM i Service.

Now that you have a basic feel for what's offered on this menu, let's take a look at a couple of the utilities available on the SECTOOLS menu. Back on the first page of this menu (Figure 14.1), options 2-4 provide a utility that will disable profiles after xx days of inactivity, where xx is a number of days you specify when taking menu option 4. You can also eliminate profiles from ever being disabled by specifying them via menu option 3. Profiles already removed from consideration are listed by taking option 2. (If you press F1 (Help) for this menu option, you'll find the list of IBM-supplied profiles already omitted from consideration.) Once you take menu option 4 to set the number of days, the job, QSECIDL1, is scheduled in the basic job scheduler to run just after midnight. This daily job will evaluate all profiles, minus the ones specified in menu option 2, and disables them based first by examining the Last used date (not the last Sign-on date), then Creation date, and finally, the Restore date of the profile. If you have no tools in place to "age" profiles (that is, disable them after a period of inactivity), this is a good (and free!) tool to get you started. However, before implementing, you'll definitely want to do analysis of the profiles that will be disabled; otherwise, be prepared to re-enable profiles that shouldn't be disabled the day after starting up this utility!

Options 5 and 6 allow you to specify profiles to disable/re-enable on a specified schedule. For example, perhaps you have vendors that you know should only be accessing the system Monday–Friday from 8:00–5:00. You can use this feature to disable the profiles when they shouldn't be on the system and enable them just prior to working hours.

Options 7 and 8 allow you to disable or delete a profile on a specific date. For example, if you create a profile and you know it's only going to be used for the next week, you can take menu option 8 and specify to delete or disable the profile on a specific date. This function is similar to what was added to the Create/Change User Profile (CRT/CHGUSRPRF) commands several releases ago except that the commands support only disabling (not deleting) profiles. Also, the CRT/CHGUSRPRF commands are slightly more flexible in that you can specify that the profile should be disabled on a specific date or after xx days. For example, you can specify to disable the profile in 30 days.

```
CRTUSRPRF USRPRF(NEWPROFILE) PASSWORD() USREXPDATE(*USREXPITV)
    USREXPITV(30)
```

I hesitate to even mention these next options, but someone might scroll down and find them, so I'll go ahead and explain their function. At the end of this menu are options 60, Configure system security, and 61, Revoke public authority to objects. DO NOT RUN THESE OPTIONS! If you do, I can say with 100% certainty that something will break. The better approach is to discover what would be set and consider setting them manually, but *do not* run the programs as shipped by IBM. Rather, run the Retrieve CL Source (RTVCLSRC) command against QSYS/QSECCFGS to determine what settings are changed by option 60 and against QSYS/QSECRVKP to determine what commands will be set to *PUBLIC *EXCLUDE. This information can also be found in Appendix G of the *IBM i Security Reference* manual. Use this information as guidelines for what to secure. But *always* determine what will break *prior* to securing commands or changing system values so that you can make an informed decision on whether or not to make the change.

Option 62, Check object integrity, is an option (or the command CHKOBJITG) that *should* be run periodically. Think of it as a self-check for the operating system. It will verify the signature, owner object domain and state, and more for operating system objects. This command can consume resources, however, so I'd run it in a batch job and at a low priority.

Reducing the Time of Your SAVSECDTA

Saving your IBM i security data is a critical part of being able to recover your system, but when it starts to take too long, you may be tempted to stop this process. Don't do it! It's likely that it's an accumulation of private authorities that's causing the issue. Let me explain.

What's Saved When You Run Save Security Data (SAVSECDTA)?

To understand how to reduce the time to run SAVSECDTA, you first need to understand what's saved during this process. When running SAVSECDTA, all user profiles, authorization lists, and private authorities are saved. How often you run SAVSECDTA depends on how often you're creating, changing, or deleting profiles; granting or revoking private authorities; or modifying authorization lists. Unless you have a record of every addition or change you've made since the last time you ran SAVSECDTA, you will need to run SAVSECDTA often, probably nightly.

Early on, running SAVSECDTA required the system to be in restricted state, but that requirement was lifted some time ago. For many organizations, running SAVSECDTA nightly makes the most sense—that is, until it starts to take longer and longer and eventually gets to the point it hasn't finished when you come in the next morning. That was the plight of one of my clients when they asked for help. Here are four steps for reducing your SAVSECDTA time.

Step 1: Delete Unused Profiles

Here's yet another reason for removing unused profiles from your system rather than just setting them to status of *DISABLED. Unless the application you're running has a hard requirement that all profiles (even inactive ones) remain on the system for historical reporting purposes, there is no reason to keep old profiles. Those old profiles pose a security risk. The risk is that they will be re-enabled and used. And because the original person assigned to any given profile is either no longer with the organization or doesn't require access to the system, the profile's use will go unnoticed.

Chapter 5 describes techniques for discovering unused profiles.

Step 2: Delete Unused Authorization Lists

Since the SAVSECDTA process saves authorization lists (as it does with unused profiles), you'll want to delete unused authorization lists. You might be tempted to delete an authorization list if it doesn't secure any objects, but I caution you not to delete it without first doing some investigation. Some applications use authorization lists to control access to a function. In fact, the operating system does this with the QPWFSERVER authorization list. (Authority to this list allows the user to see the QSYS.LIB file system in Windows Explorer and Access Client Solutions interfaces.) And you may want to use an authorization list in IBM i 7.5 to limit who can use a file share. Again, that's why it's so important to make the description meaningful. Bottom line: Prior to deleting an authorization list, first determine if it's being used in this manner.

Step 3: Consider Using Authorization Lists

If you have granted the same private authority to many objects, consider attaching an authorization list to the objects, granting the appropriate private authority to the authorization list, and removing the private authorities granted to the individual objects. For example, perhaps you've granted GRPPGMR *USE authority and ODBCAPP *CHANGE authority to all physical files in your application libraries. This would amount to the system having to save two private authorities for every database member plus one for the cursor multiplied by the number of files multiplied by 2 (for the authority to GRPPGMR and ODBCAPP). That's a lot of private authorities being saved! Contrast that with using authorization lists. That way, the system is saving only two private authorities: The authorities (GRPPGMR and ODBCAPP) have been granted to the authorization list. Depending on how many files and whether the files are multi-member, this could be a huge difference.

Step 4: Find and Remove Unnecessary Private Authorities

Next, the scenario that my client found themselves in: a growing number of private authorities. They could tell by using performance tools that the part of the SAVSECDTA process that was taking the longest was when private authorities were being saved. But they had no idea how to determine to whom and to which objects the authorities had been granted. To determine this, they ran Print Profile Internals (PRTPRFINT). This command produces a report that lists how "full" a profile is. Let me explain what I mean by that.

Profiles contain attributes such as initial program, initial menu, output queue, etc., but the *USRPRF object also contains other information. Specifically, *USRPRF objects contain an entry for every object the profile owns, an entry for every private authority granted to it, an entry for every private authority granted to one of its owned objects, and an entry for every object for which it's been made the primary group profile. There is a limit to the size of the user profile object, and it's these entries that contribute to that size. Back in the late Version 4 and Version 5 releases, it was fairly easy to reach the limit, especially if one profile owned most of the objects on the system and it was one of the larger iSeries systems. Running the PRTPRFINT command allowed you to monitor how full profiles were getting and use that to avoid situations where applications failed because the application profile couldn't own more objects. Today, the maximum size of the user profile object has been increased so much that it's very difficult to reach the limit (although it's still possible). Even so, the PRTPRFINT still yields interesting information, especially when you're trying to determine why a SAVSECDTA operation is taking a long time.

When prompting the PRTPRFINT command, you can specify that you want all profiles or only profiles that are greater than a specific percentage full. I usually run the report looking for profiles greater than 2% full. Yes, just 2%. Sometimes, you'll get a report with lots of profiles just over 2% full, but usually, you'll see that 2–5 profiles are the culprits; those are profiles that have a large number of private authority entries, typically 5–10% full of private authority entries. Often, they're either administrator profiles or service accounts.

Now that you've identified the profiles, you have to determine what objects they've been authorized to. Enter the Work with Objects by Private Auth (WRKOBJPVT) command. This command lists all of the objects, including IFS objects, to which the user has been granted a private authority. About 95% of the time, the issue will be that the profile has private authorities to hundreds if not thousands of IFS objects. Now the trick is to determine how that's happening and whether the user even needs authority to the objects. If they do, then you need to determine how they're going to continue to have access but via some means other than a private authority. What you'll often find is that subdirectories have been created by a different administrator than the directory, and the original creator now has a private authority to the subdirectories and everything in them. In this case, the way to correct the issue is to remove the unnecessary private authorities from the subdirectory where the objects are being created. The objects will no longer be created with the excess private authorities.

Let's look at an example. You've found via analyzing the output of PRTPVTAUT that profiles Alex, Scott, and Geoffrey are the "fullest" profiles on the system. Running the WRKPVTAUT commands against the Alex and Scott profiles shows that they have a private authority to each invoice stored in the /Company/Product/AR_App directory. How is this happening? A closer look at the ownership of these directories reveals that Alex originally created the /Company directory, but Scott created the /Company/Product directory. Because subdirectories inherit the authority from its parent, the system grants Alex a private authority to the /Company/Product directory. Later, the AR_App directory was created to hold archived invoices. That directory was created by Geoffrey, so now both Alex and Scott have a private authority to the /Company/Product/AR_App directory. Objects (the invoices) are written to this directory via a nightly scheduled job running as Ted. Whenever a new invoice is created, the system grants Alex, Scott, and Geoffrey a private authority to the stream file (*STMF) storing the invoice.

Now that you've found the source of the issue, how do you resolve it? The easiest way to resolve this is to make Ted the owner of the /Company/Product/AR_App directory, making sure to take the option to revoke the current owner's (in this case, Geoffrey's) authority, as well as removing the private authorities granted to Alex and Scott. New invoices will only have Ted's owner authority and *PUBLIC authority, eliminating the unnecessary private authorities.

Some organizations have a similar application and will keep a rolling 60 or 90 days' worth of information. If that's the case, you may choose to simply let the invoices with the extra private authorities age off the system. However, if this is a true archive and the number is continuing to increase, you may want to remove the excess private authorities by running the Change Authority (CHGAUT) command. The following removes the private authorities granted to Alex to both /Company/Product/AR_App directory as well as all objects in the directory.

```
CHGAUT OBJ('/Company/Product/AR_App') USER(ALEX) DTAAUT(*NONE)
OBJAUT(*NONE) SUBTREE(*ALL)
```

I've seen several variations of this issue, but this discovery technique has allowed me to resolve them all.

Note

The authority granted to the owner of an object does *not* count as a private authority! Rather, it's an ownership entry in the *USRPRF; therefore, you shouldn't remove owners' authority. In fact, removing owners' authority to IFS objects can cause subsequent objects to be created without the owner having Object Authorities, causing some hard-to-debug operational issues (strange but true.)

The Value of Saving Time

What I never stated but I hope is understood is that reducing the time for SAVSECDTA to run also reduces the time it will take should you ever have to restore your system. It should go without saying that you don't want to have to waste your time restoring unneeded profiles, authorization lists, or authorities when all you want to do is get your organization back up and running.

The Audit Journal as an Early Warning System

I've provided several examples of using the information in the audit journal throughout this book, and chapter 15 in *IBM i Security Administration and Compliance, Third Edition* describes how to configure auditing as well as various ways to use the information. But I wanted to make sure that I discuss ways to use it as an early warning signal of an attack. Neglecting this information in the IBM i audit journal is a lost opportunity for getting an early warning that something is amiss in your network.

Specifically, three types of entries, if detected, should cause alarm bells to go off:

- PW: Password entries, specifically PW with a subtype of U (indicating that the profile name is invalid). If you see entries where the user name is ADMIN or ROOT, this should send a warning. That's because these are two well-known user names: ADMIN for Windows and ROOT for UNIX/Linux. Never should they be valid users on your system running IBM i. Intruders will often probe systems using weak passwords for these administrative accounts, hoping to gain access. But you can use it as an early warning signal that someone has gained access to your network. Be aware: If you have software that regularly probes your network for vulnerabilities, you'll want to exclude that server's IP address from your query so you don't sound an alarm for known (and approved) activity.

To generate PW entries, you must have *AUTFAIL specified for the QAUDLVL system value and *AUDLVL included in QAUDCTL.

- JS: If you see a JS (Job Start) entry where the IP address is an external IP address that is unknown to you, sound the alarm. I know many of you will have a process that comes in from an external IP address, especially if your system is communicating with a server in the cloud. But these should be well-known addresses having a specific firewall rule allowing it into your network. That's why, if you see an external IP address that's not one you're familiar with, you'd better quickly investigate. Likely this is an indication that your firewall has either failed or had a rule put in place that has opened your network to the internet.

To generate JS entries, you must specify either *JOBBAS or *JOBDTA in QAUDLVL and specify *AUDLVL in QAUDCTL. I've already warned you in earlier chapters that this auditing feature generates *a lot* of entries. But if your system can handle the extra volume, the JS entries can tell you a lot.

- IM: The Intrusion Detection feature of IBM i can alert you to issues at the TCP/IP stack layer (malformed packets, syn attacks, etc.). Once enabled and configured, I've seen this feature alert administrators that malware, especially cryptomining software, has entered into their network.

Configuring Intrusion Detection is a two-step process. You must add *ATNEVT to the QAUDLVL system value (along with *AUDLVL in QAUDCTL) and then you must go into Navigator and do additional configuration to specify which issues you wish to be alerted on and to whom the alerts are to be sent. For more information, search for the Security Intrusion Detection manual that corresponds to the version of the operating system you're running.